Thomas Nettleship Staley

The Hawaiian Hymnal

Being Hymns For Use In The Diocese Of Honolulu

Thomas Nettleship Staley

The Hawaiian Hymnal
Being Hymns For Use In The Diocese Of Honolulu

ISBN/EAN: 9783744651424

Printed in Europe, USA, Canada, Australia, Japan

Cover: Foto ©ninafisch / pixelio.de

More available books at **www.hansebooks.com**

THE HAWAIIAN HYMNAL,

BEING

HYMNS

FOR USE IN THE DIOCESE OF

HONOLULU.

"Let every thing that hath breath PRAISE THE LORD."

HONOLULU:
1862.

NOTE.

The Hawaiian Hymnal will be published in three parts :

Part I. containing Hymns for use from Advent to Lent ;

Part II., from Lent to Trinity ;

Part III., from Trinity to Advent.

IMPRIMATUR.

This Hymnal having received sanction of the Synod, I hereby constitute it for use in my Diocese of Honolulu.

† T. N., HONOLULU.

HYMNS.

BAPTISM.

"Buried with Him in Baptism."

1. With Christ we share a mystic grave,
   With Christ we buried lie;
   But 'tis not in the darksome cave
   By mournful Calvary.

   The pure and bright Baptismal flood
   Entombs our nature's stain;
   New creatures from the cleansing wave
   With Christ we rise again.

   Thrice blest, if through this world of sin,
   And lust, and selfish care,
   Our resurrection-mantle white
   And undefiled we wear.

   Thrice blest, if, through the gate of death,
   Glorious at last and free,
   We to our joyful rising pass,
   O Risen Lord, with Thee.   Amen.

"The washing of regeneration."

2   'Tis done; that new and heavenly birth
Which re-creates the sons of earth,
And cleanses from the guilt of sin
The souls whom JESUS died to win.

'Tis done; the Cross upon the brow
Is marked for weal or sorrow now;
To shine with Heavenly lustre bright,
Or burn in everlasting night.

O ye who brought that babe to-day
Within a SAVIOUR'S arms to lie,
Watch well and guard with careful eye
The heir of immortality.

Teach it to know a FATHER's love,
And seek for happiness above,
To CHRIST its heart and treasure give,
And in the SPIRIT ever live.

That so before the judgment-seat
In joy and triumph we may meet;
The battle fought, the struggle o'er,
The Kingdom your's for evermore.

Praise GOD from whom all blessings flow,
Praise Him, all creatures here below;
Praise Him above, ye heavenly host;
Praise FATHER, SON, and HOLY GHOST.
                      Amen.

CONFIRMATION.

" When Thou lettest thy Breath go forth they shall be made, and Thou shalt renew the face of the earth."

3. Come, Thou Holy Spirit, come;
And from Thine eternal home
   Shed the ray of light divine;
Come, Thou Father of the poor,
Come, Thou source of all our store,
   Come, within our bosoms shine.

Thou of Comforters the best,
Thou the soul's most welcome Guest,
   Sweet Refreshment here below!
In our labour rest most sweet,
Grateful shadow from the heat,
   Solace in the midst of woe!

O most Blessed Light Divine,
Shine within these hearts of Thine,
   And our inmost being fill:
If Thou take Thy grace away,
Nothing pure in man will stay,
   All our good is turned to ill.

Heal our wounds; our strength renew;
On our dryness pour Thy dew;
   Wash the stains of guilt away:
Bend the stubborn heart and will,
Melt the frozen, warm the chill,
   Guide the steps that go astray.

On the faithful, who adore
And confess Thee, evermore
  In Thy sevenfold gifts descend;
Give them virtue's sure reward,
Give them Thy salvation, LORD,
  Give them joys that never end.
                   Amen.

"It shall come to pass in the last days, saith God, I will pour out of My Spirit upon all flesh."

4.   Come, HOLY GHOST, our souls inspire,
And lighten with celestial fire;
Thou the anointing SPIRIT art,
Who dost thy sevenfold Gifts impart;

Thy blessed Unction from above
Is comfort, life, and fire of love.
Enable with perpetual light
The dulness of our blinded sight;

Anoint and cheer our soiled face
With the abundance of Thy Grace:
Keep far our foes, give peace at home;
Where thou art Guide, no ill can come.

Teach us to know the FATHER, SON,
And THEE, of BOTH, to be but ONE;
That, through the ages all along,
This may be our endless song;
Praise to Thy eternal merit,
FATHER, SON, and HOLY SPIRIT. Amen.

HOLY EUCHARIST.

" Do This in remembrance of Me."

5.   Sing we that Blest Body broken,
     Our weak souls' mysterious Food;
And the words our King hath spoken,
     Gifting us with His own blood,
His true presence to betoken,
     And our holy brotherhood.

Born for us, and for us given,
     Of a virgin undefil'd,
Scattering precious seed from Heaven,
     Sojourn'd He in this world's wild;
On that much-remember'd even,
     He His wondrous course fulfill'd.

Meekly to the law complying,
     He had finish'd its commands;
And to them at supper lying
     Gave Himself with His own Hands;
A memorial of His dying,
     Thenceforth unto all the lands.

God the Word by one word maketh
     Bread His very Flesh to be;
And whoso that Cup partaketh
     Tastes the Fount of Calvary:
While the carnal mind forsaketh,
     Faith receives, the Mystery.

Unto this His Presence veiled
  Draw we nigh, with heads bow'd low:
All that Paschal rites entailed
  Yields to higher blessings now;
Earthly touch and sight have failed—
  Faith adores, nor questions how.

Power ascribe we, praise and blessing,
  Both to FATHER and to SON:
HOLY SPIRIT, Thee addressing,
  One with Them, as LORD alone:
This right faith we hold, confessing
  Persons Three in Substance One.
                            Amen.

"Come, for all things are now ready."

6. MY GOD, and is Thy table spread,
And doth Thy cup with love o'erflow?
Thither be all Thy children led,
And let them all Thy sweetness know.

Hail, sacred Feast, which JESUS makes,
Rich banquet of His Flesh and Blood!
Thrice happy he who here partakes
That sacred stream, that heavenly food.

Why are its dainties all in vain
Before unwilling hearts displayed?
Was not for them the Victim slain?
Are they forbid the children's bread?

O let Thy table honoured be,
And furnished well with joyful guests;
And may each soul salvation see
That here its sacred pledges tastes.

To FATHER, SON, and HOLY GHOST,
The GOD Whom heaven and earth adore,
From men and from the angel-host
Be praise and glory evermore.   Amen.

"JESUS said unto them, I am the Bread of Life."

7.   THEE we adore, O hidden SAVIOUR, Thee,
Who in Thy Sacrament dost deign to be;
Both flesh and spirit at Thy presence fail,
Yet here thy presence we devoutly hail.

O blest Memorial of our dying LORD,
Who living Bread to men doth here afford!
O may our souls for ever feed on Thee,
And Thou, O CHRIST, for ever precious be.

Fountain of Goodness, JESU, LORD and GOD,
Cleanse us unclean, with Thy most cleansing blood;
Increase our faith and love, that we may know
The hope and peace which from Thy presence flow.

O CHRIST, Whom now beneath a veil we see,
May what we thirst for soon our portion be,
To gaze on Thee, and see with unveiled face
The vision of Thy glory and Thy grace.
       Amen.

"My Flesh is meat indeed, and my Blood is drink indeed."

8. O GOD, unseen yet ever near,
  Thy presence may we feel;
And, thus inspired with holy fear,
  Before Thine altar kneel.

Here may Thy faithful people know
  The blessings of Thy love,
The streams that through the desert flow,
  The manna from above.

We come, obedient to Thy word,
  To feast on heavenly Food;
Our meat, the Body of the LORD,
  Our drink, His precious Blood.

Thus may we all Thy words obey,
  For we, O GOD, are Thine;
And go rejoicing on our way,
  Renewed with strength divine.

To FATHER, SON, and HOLY GHOST,
  The GOD Whom we adore,
Be glory, as it was, is now,
  And shall be evermore. Amen.

SUNDAY MORNING.

"In Thy Light shall we see light."

9. Morn of morns, and day of days!
Silent as the new-born rays,
From the sepulchre's dark prison
Christ, the Light of lights, is risen.

He commanded, and His word
Death and the dread chaos heard;
O shall we, more deaf than they,
In the chains of darkness stay?

Nature yet in shadow lies,
Let the sons of light arise
And prevent the morning rays
With sweet canticles of praise.

While the dead world sleeps around,
Let the sacred temples sound
Law, and prophet, and blest psalm
Lit with holy light so calm.

Unto hearts in slumber weak
Let the heavenly trumpet speak;
And a heavenward walk express
Our new life to holiness.

Hear us, Lord, and with us be,
O Thou Fount of charity,
Thou Who dost the Spirit give,
Bidding the dead letter live.

Glory to the FATHER, SON,
And to Thee, O HOLY ONE,
By Whose quickening Breath divine
Our dull spirits burn and shine.   Amen.

"Blessing, and glory, and wisdom, and thanksgiving, and honour, and power, and might, be unto our GOD for ever and ever.   Amen."

10. ON this the day that saw the earth
From utter darkness first have birth;—
The day its Maker rose again,
And vanquish'd death, and burst our chain:

Away with sleep and slothful ease!
We raise our hearts and bend our knees,
And early seek the Lord of all,
According to the prophet's call.

That He may grant us that we crave;
May stretch His strong right arm to save;
And, purging out each sinful stain,
Restore us to our Home again.

Assembled here this holy day,
This holiest hour we raise the lay:
And oh that He to Whom we sing
May now reward our offering!

O Father of unclouded light!
We pray Thee, kneeling in Thy sight,
From all defilement to be freed,
And every sinful act and deed:

That this our body's mortal frame
May know no sin, and fear no shame,
Whereby the fires of hell may rise
To torture us in fiercer wise.

We therefore, Saviour, cry to Thee
To wash out our iniquity:
And give us of Thy boundless grace
The blessings of the Heav'nly Place.

That we, thence exil'd by our sin,
Hereafter may be welcom'd in:
That blessed time awaiting now,
With hymns of glory here we bow.

O Father, that we ask be done,
Through JESUS CHRIST, Thine Only Son;
Who, with the Holy Ghost and Thee,
Shall live and reign eternally. Amen.

SUNDAY EVENING.

"Behold, He That keepeth Israel shall neither slumber nor sleep."

11. BE present, Holy Father,
    Unseen by mortal eye;
And CHRIST the Word Eternal,
    And Spirit from on high!

Thou Trinity, in Essence
    And light and virtue One:
Father, and Son, and Spirit
    Of Father and of Son:

The toil of day is over;
   The hour of rest comes round:
And in its turn kind slumber
   Our members hath unbound.

Servant of CHRIST, remember
   The Font's Baptismal dew:
Remember thy renewal
   In Confirmation too.

And thou, O crafty serpent,
   Who seek'st by many an art,
And many a guileful winding,
   To vex the quiet heart:

Depart, for CHRIST is present:
   Since CHRIST is here, give place:
And let the sign thou ownest
   Thy ghostly legions chase.

And though awhile the body
   In sleep may lie reclined,
Yet CHRIST, in very slumber,
   Shall fill the Christian mind.

All laud to GOD the Father,
   All laud to GOD the Son;
To GOD the Holy Spirit
   Be equal honours done.   Amen.

MORNING HYMN.

"Now unto the King eternal, immortal, invisible, the only wise God, be honour and glory for ever and ever. Amen."

12.   Now that the daylight fills the sky,
      We lift our hearts to GOD on high,
That He, in all we do, or say,
Would keep us free from harm to-day:

Would guard our hearts and tongues from strife;
From anger's din would hide our life:
From all ill sights would turn our eyes:
Would close our ears from vanities:

Would keep our inmost conscience pure:
Our souls from folly would secure:
Would bid us check the pride of sense
With due and holy abstinence.

So we, when this new day is gone,
And night in turn is drawing on,
With conscience by the world unstained,
Shall praise His Name for vict'ry gained.

All laud to GOD the Father be;
All praise, Eternal Son, to Thee;
All praise for ever, as is meet,
To GOD the Holy Paraclete.   Amen.

"Let us go up to the mountain of the Lord, to the house of the God of Jacob; and He will teach us of His ways, and we will walk in His paths: for out of Zion shall go forth the law, and the word of the Lord from Jerusalem."

13. Our limbs refresh'd with slumber now,
    And sloth cast off, in prayer we bow:
    And while we sing Thy praises dear,
    O Father, be Thou present here!

    To Thee our earliest morning song,
    To Thee our hearts' full powers belong:
    And Thou, O Holy One, prevent
    Each following action and intent.

    As shades at morning flee away,
    And night before the Star of day,
    So each transgression of the night
    Be purg'd by Thee, celestial Light!

    Cut off, we pray Thee, each offence,
    And every lust of thought and sense;
    That by their lips who Thee adore
    Thou may'st be prais'd for evermore.

    O Father, that we ask be done,
    Through JESUS CHRIST, Thine Only Son;
    Who, with the Holy Ghost and Thee,
    Shall live and reign eternally.   Amen.

"I myself will awake right early."

14. Awake, my soul, and with the sun
Thy daily stage of duty run;
Shake off dull sloth, and early rise
To pay thy morning sacrifice.

Redeem thy mis-spent moments past,
And live this day as if thy last;
Improve thy talent with due care,
For the great day thyself prepare.

Let all thy converse be sincere,
Thy conscience as the noon-day clear;
Think how all-seeing God thy ways
And all thy secret thoughts surveys.

By influence of the Light divine
Let thy own light to others shine,
Reflect all heaven's propitious rays
In ardent love and cheerful praise.

Part II.

Wake and lift up thyself, my heart,
And with the angels bear thy part,
Who all night long unwearied sing
High praise to their Eternal King.

I wake, I wake, ye heavenly choir,
May your devotion me inspire,
That I like you my age may spend,
Like you may on my God attend.

May I like you in God delight,
Have all day long my God in sight,
Perform like you my Maker's will,
O may I never more do ill.

Had I your wings to heaven I'd fly,
But God shall that defect supply,
And my soul, winged with warm desire,
Shall all day long to heaven aspire.

Part III.

Glory to Thee Who safe has kept
And hast refreshed me while I slept;
Grant, Lord, when I from death shall wake,
I may of endless light partake.

I would not wake, nor rise again,
E'en heaven itself I would disdain,
Wert Thou not there to be enjoyed,
And I in hymns to be employed.

Heaven is, dear Lord, where'er Thou art,
O never then from me depart;
For to my soul 'tis hell to be
But for one moment without Thee.

Lord, I my vows to Thee renew,
Scatter my sins as morning dew;
Guard my first springs of thought and will,
And with Thyself my spirit fill.

Direct, control, suggest this day
All I design, or do, or say;
That all my powers with all their might
In Thy sole glory may unite.

Doxology to be sung at the end of each Part.

Praise GOD, from Whom all blessings flow;
Praise Him, all creatures here below;
Praise Him above, ye Heavenly host;
Praise FATHER, SON, and HOLY GHOST.
                              Amen.

EVENING HYMN.

15. ALL praise to Thee, my GOD, this night
For all the blessings of the light;
Keep me, O keep me, King of kings,
Beneath Thine own Almighty wings.

Forgive me, LORD, for Thy dear SON,
The ill that I this day have done,
That with the world, myself, and Thee,
I, ere I sleep, at peace may be.

Teach me to live, that I may dread
The grave as little as my bed;
To die, that this vile body may
Rise glorious at the awful Day.

O may my soul on Thee repose,
And may sweet sleep mine eyelids close,
Sleep that may me more vig'rous make
To serve my GOD when I awake.

When in the night I sleepless lie,
My soul with Heavenly thoughts supply;
Let no ill dreams disturb my rest,
No power of darkness me molest.

O may my Guardian, while I sleep,
Close to my bed his vigils keep,
His love angelical instill,
Stop all the avenues of ill.

May he celestial joys rehearse,
And thought to thought with me converse;
Or in my stead, all the night long,
Sing to my GOD a grateful song.

Praise GOD from Whom all blessings flow;
Praise him all creatures here below;
Praise Him above, ye heavenly host;
Praise FATHER, SON, and HOLY GHOST.
Amen.

"Abide with us."

16. SUN of my soul, Thou SAVIOUR dear,
It is not night if Thou be near;
O may no earth-born cloud arise
To hide Thee from Thy servant's eyes.

When the soft dews of kindly sleep
My wearied eyelids gently steep,
Be my last thought, how sweet to rest
For ever on my SAVIOUR's breast.

Abide with me from morn till eve,
For without Thee I cannot live;
Abide with me when night is nigh,
For without Thee I dare not die.

Oh! by Thine own sad burthen borne,
So meekly up the Hill of Scorn,
Teach Thou Thy Priests their daily Cross
To bear as Thine, nor count it loss.

If some poor wandering child of Thine
Have spurned to-day the voice divine,
Now, LORD, the gracious work begin;
Let him no more lie down in sin.

Watch by the sick; enrich the poor
With blessings from Thy boundless store;
Be every mourner's sleep to-night,
Like infant's slumbers, pure and light.

Come near and bless us when we wake,
Ere through the world our way we take;
Till in the ocean of Thy love
We lose ourselves in Heaven above.
Amen.

"He giveth His Beloved, sleep."

17. THE day is past and gone;
    Great GOD, we bow to Thee;
Again, as shades of night come on,
    Unto Thy side we flee.

O, when shall that day come,
  Ne'er sinking in the west,
That country, and that holy home,
  Where none shall break our rest?

Where all things shall be peace,
  And joyance without end,
And golden harps that never cease,
  With echoing lips shall blend?

Blend in their sweet accord,
  Of deep, and full, and bright,
Like sounds of many waters poured
  On the tranced ear of night.

So we, preserved beneath
  The sheltering of Thy wing,
For evermore Thy praise shall breathe,
  And love Thee, LORD, and sing.

To GOD the FATHER praise,
  And to the eternal SON,
And to the HOLY GHOST always,
  Co-equal Three in One.   Amen.

"Abide with us; for it is toward evening, and the day is far spent."

18.   ABIDE with me; fast falls the even tide;
The darkness deepens; LORD, with me abide;
When other helpers fail, and comforts flee,
Help of the helpless, O abide with me.

Swift to its close ebbs out life's little day;
Earth's joys grow dim, its glories pass away;
Change and decay in all around I see ;
O Thou Who changest not, abide with me.

I need Thy presence every passing hour ;
What but Thy grace can foil the tempter's
    power?
Who like Thyself my gu de and stay can be?
Through cloud and sunshine, LORD, abide
    with me.

I fear no foe with Thee at hand to bless ;
Ills have no weight, and tears no bitterness;
Where is death's sting, where, grave, thy
    victory?
I triumph still, if Thou abide with me.

Hold Thou Thy Cross before my closing eyes;
Shine through the gloom, and point me to the
    skies;
Heaven's morning breaks, and earth's vain
    shadows flee;
In life, in death, O LORD, abide with me.
                           Amen.

SATURDAY EVENING.

"There remaineth therefore a rest to the people of God."

19. O what their joy
    and their glory must be;—
Those endless Sabbaths
    the blessed ones see!
Crown for the valiant:
    to weary ones rest:
God shall be all,
    and in all ever blest.

What are the Monarch,
    His court and His throne?
What are the peace
    and the joy that they own?
Tell us, ye blest ones,
    that in it have share,
If what ye feel
    ye can fully declare.

Truly "Jerusalem"
    name we that shore,
"Vision of Peace"
    that brings joy evermore!
Wish and fulfillment
    can sever'd be ne'er;
Nor the thing pray'd for
    come short of the prayer.

We, where no trouble
   distraction can bring,
Safely the anthems
   of Sion shall sing:
While for Thy grace, LORD,
   their voices of praise
Thy blessed people
   shall evermore raise.

There dawns no Sabbath,
   no Sabbath is o'er;
Those Sabbath-keepers
   have one, and no more;
One and unending
   is that triumph-song
Which to the Angels
   and us shall belong.

Now in the meanwhile,
   with hearts raised on high,
We for that Country
   must yearn and must sigh:
Seeking Jerusalem,
   dear native land,
Through our long exile
   on Babylon's strand.

Lowly before Him
   with praises we fall,
Of Whom, and *in* Whom,
   and *through* Whom are all:
Of Whom,—the Father;
   in Whom,—the Son;
Through Whom,—the Spirit,
   with These ever One.   Amen.

ADVENT.

20. The Advent of our God
 Our prayers must now employ,
And we must meet Him on His road
 With hymns of holy joy.

The everlasting Son
 A Maiden's Offspring see,
A servant's form He putteth on
 To make His people free.

Daughter of Sion, rise
 And greet Thy lowly King!
And do not wickedly despise
 The mercies He will bring.

As Judge, in clouds of light
 He will come down again,
And all His scattered saints unite,
 With Him in Heaven to reign.

Before that dreadful day
 May all our sins be gone!
May the old man be put away,
 And the new man put on.

Praise to the Saviour Son,
 Who came to seek the lost;
Like praise be to the Father done,
 And to the Holy Ghost.   Amen.

" Now it is high time to awake out of sleep."

21. Hark! a thrilling voice is sounding;
    " Christ is nigh," it seems to say;
    " Cast away the dreams of darkness,
    O ye children of the day!"

Wakened by the solemn warning,
  Let the earth-bound soul arise;
Christ, her Sun, all ill dispelling,
  Shines upon the morning skies.

Lo! the Lamb, so long expected,
  Comes with pardon down from heaven;
Let us haste, with tears of sorrow,
  One and all to be forgiven:

That when next He comes with glory
  And the world is wrapped in fear,
With His mercy He may shield us,
  And with words of love draw near.

Honour, glory, might, and blessing
  To the Father and the Son,
With the Everlasting Spirit,
  While eternal ages run.   Amen.

" Now it is high time to awake out of sleep: for now is our salvation nearer than when we believed."

22. To earth descending, Word sublime,
    Begotten ere the days of time,
    Who cam'st a Child, the world to aid,
    As years their downward course display'd:

Each breast be light'ned from above,
Each heart be kindled with Thy love;
That we, who hear Thy call to-day,
At length may cast earth's joys away:

That so,—when Thou, our Judge, art nigh,
All secret deeds of men to try,
Shalt mete to sin pangs rightly won,
To just men joy for deeds well done,—

Thy servants may not be enchain'd
By punishment their guilt has gain'd:
But with the blessed evermore
May serve and love Thee, and adore.

To Him Who comes the world to free,
To GOD the SON, all glory be:
To GOD the FATHER, as is meet,
To GOD the Blessed Paraclete.   Amen.

"The great and terrible day of the LORD."

23.   DAY of wrath!   O day of mourning!
See! once more the Cross returning—
Heav'n and earth in ashes burning!

O what fear man's bosom rendeth,
When from heav'n the Judge descendeth,
On Whose sentence all dependeth!

Wondrous sound the trumpet flingeth,
Through earth's sepulchres it ringeth,
All before the throne it bringeth!

Death is struck, and nature quaking—
All creation is awaking,
To its Judge an answer making!

Lo, the Book exactly worded!
Wherein all hath been recorded;—
Thence shall judgment be awarded.

When the Judge His seat attaineth,
And each hidden deed arraigneth,
Nothing unaveng'd remaineth.

What shall I, frail man, be pleading?
Who for me be interceding?—
When the just are mercy needing.

King of majesty tremendous,
Who dost free salvation send us,
Fount of pity! then befriend us!

Think! kind Jesu—my salvation
Caus'd Thy wondrous Incarnation;
Leave me not to reprobation!

Faint and weary Thou hast sought me,
On the Cross of suffering bought me;—
Shall such grace be vainly brought me?

Righteous Judge of retribution,
Grant Thy gift of absolution,
Ere that reckoning-day's conclusion.

Guilty, now I pour my moaning,
All my shame with anguish owning;
Spare, O GOD, Thy suppliant, groaning!

Thou, the sinful woman savest—
Thou, the dying thief forgavest;
And to me a hope vouchsafest!

Worthless are my prayers and sighing,
Yet, good LORD, in grace complying,
Rescue me from fires undying!

With Thy favour'd sheep, O place me!
Nor among the goats abase me;
But to Thy right hand upraise me.

While the wicked are confounded,
Doom'd to flames of woe unbounded,
Call me! with Thy saints surrounded.

Low I kneel, with heart-submission;
See, like ashes, my contrition—
Help me, in my last condition!

Ah! that Day of tears and mourning!
From the dust of earth returning,

Man for judgment must prepare him;—
Spare! O GOD, in mercy spare him!

LORD, Who didst our souls redeem,
Grant a blessed requiem! Amen.

"The Lord himself shall descend from heaven with a shout, with the voice of the archangel, and with the trump of God."

24. Great God, what do I see and hear?
   The end of things created:
Thu Judge of all men doth appear
   On clouds of glory seated;
The trumpet sounds, the graves restore
The dead which they contained before;
   Prepare, my soul, to meet Him.

The dead in Christ are first to rise,
   At that last trumpet's sounding;
Caught up to meet Him in the skies,
   With joy their Lord surrounding;
No gloomy fears their souls dismay;
His presence sheds eternal day
   On those prepared to meet Him.

The ungodly, filled with guilty fears,
   Behold His wrath prevailing;
In woe they rise, but all their tears
   And sighs are unavailing;
The day of grace is past and gone;
Trembling they stand before His throne,
   All unprepared to meet Him.

Great Judge, to Thee our prayers we pour,
   In deep abasement bending;
O shield us through that last dread hour,
   Thy wondrous love extending:
May we, in this our trial day,
With faithful hearts Thy word obey,
   And thus prepare to meet Thee. Amen.

"He hath sent Me to bind up the broken-hearted, to proclaim liberty to the captives."

25. Hark the glad sound! the Saviour comes,
The Saviour promised long :
Let every heart prepare a throne,
And every voice a song.

He comes, the prisoners to release,
In Satan's bondage held ;
The gates of brass before Him burst,
The iron fetters yield.

He comes, the broken hearts to bind,
The bleeding souls to cure,
And with the treasures of His grace
To bless the humble poor.

Our glad Hosannas, Prince of Peace,
Thine Advent shall proclaim ;
And heaven's eternal arches ring
With Thy beloved Name. Amen.

"Behold I send My messenger."

26 When Christ the Lord would come on earth,
His messenger before Him went;
The greatest born of mortal birth,
And charged with words of deep intent.

The least of all that here attend
    Hath honour greater far than he;
He was the Bridegroom's joyful friend,
    His Body and His Spouse are we.

A higher race the sons of light,
    Of Water and the Spirit born;
He the last star of parting night,
    And we the children of the morn.

And as he boldly spake Thy words,
    And joyed to hear the Bridegroom's voice,
Thus may Thy pastors teach, O LORD,
    And thus Thy listening Church rejoice!

To FATHER, SON, and HOLY GHOST,
    The GOD Whom Heaven and earth adore,
Be glory, as it was of old,
    Is now, and shall be evermore.

"Now it is high time to awake out of sleep; for now is our salvation nearer than when we believed."

27. CREATOR of the stars of night,
    Thy people's everlasting light,
    Jesu, Redeemer, save us all,
    And hear Thy servants when they call.

Thou, grieving that the ancient curse
Should doom to death an universe,
Hast found the med'cine, full of grace,
To save and heal a ruin'd race.

Thou cam'st, the Bridegroom of the Bride,
As drew the world to evening tide ;
Proceeding from a Virgin shrine,
The spotless Victim all divine.

At Whose dread Name, Majestic now,
All knees must bend, all hearts must bow ;
And things celestial Thee shall own,
And things terrestial, Lord alone.

O Thou Whose coming is with dread
To judge and doom the quick and dead,
Preserve us, while we dwell below
From ev'ry insult of the foe.

To Him, Who comes the world to free,
To God the Son, all glory be ;
To God the Father, as is meet,
To God the blessed Paraclete.   Amen.

CHRISTMAS EVE.

"When the fullness of the time was come, God sent forth his Son, made of a woman, made under the law, to redeem them that were under the law, that we might receive the adoption of sons."

28. COME, Thou Redeemer of the earth,
Come, testify Thy Virgin birth :
All lands admire,—all times applaud ;
Such is the birth that fits a God.

Begotten of no human will,
But of the Spirit, mystic still,
The Word of God, in flesh array'd,
The promis'd fruit to man display'd.

The Virgin womb that burden gain'd,
With Virgin honour all unstain'd :
The banners there of virtue glow :
God in his temple dwells below.

Proceeding from His Chamber free,
The royal hall of chastity,
Giant of twofold substance, straight
His destined way He runs elate.

From God the Father He proceeds :
To God the Father back He speeds :
Proceeds,—as far as very hell ;
Speeds back,—to light ineffable.

O Equal to Thy Father, Thou !
Gird on Thy fleshly mantle now :
The weakness of our mortal state,
With deathless might invigorate.

Thy cradle here shall glitter bright,
And darkness breathe a newer light ;
Where endless faith shall shine serene,
And twilight never intervene.

All honour, laud, and glory be,
O Jesu, Virgin-born, to Thee !
All glory, as is ever meet,
To Father and to Paraclete.   Amen.

"Unto you is born this day in the city of David a
SAVIOUR which is CHRIST the LORD."

29. WHILE shepherds watched their flocks
  by night,
 All seated on the ground,
The angel of the LORD came down,
 And glory shone around.

"Fear not," said he; for mighty dread
 Had seized their troubled mind;
"Glad tidings of great joy I bring
 To you and all mankind.

"To you in David's town this day
 Is born of David's line,
A SAVIOUR, Who is CHRIST the LORD;
 And this shall be the sign:

"The Heavenly Babe you there shall find
 To human view displayed,
All meanly wrapped in swathing bands,
 And in a manger laid."

Thus spake the seraph; and forthwith
 Appeared a shining throng,
Of angels praising GOD, who thus
 Addressed their joyful song:

"All glory be to GOD on high,
 And in the earth be peace;
Good will henceforth from Heaven to men
 Begin and never cease." Amen.

CHRISTMAS.

"Glory to God in the highest, and on earth peace, good will toward men."

30. Hark! the herald-angels sing
Glory to the new-born KING,
Peace on earth, and mercy mild,
God and sinners reconciled.
Joyful, all ye nations, rise,
Join the triumph of the skies;
With the angelic host proclaim
Christ is born in Bethlehem.
 Hark! the herald-angels sing
 Glory to the new-born KING.

Christ, by highest heaven adored,
Christ, the everlasting Lord,
Late in time behold Him come,
Offspring of a Virgin's womb.
Veiled in flesh the Godhead see!
Hail, the Incarnate Deity!
Pleased as Man with man to dwell,
Jesus, our Emmanuel.
 Hark! the herald-angels sing
 Glory to the new-born King.

Hail the heaven-born Prince of Peace!
Hail, the Sun of Righteousness!
Light and Life to all He brings.
Risen with healing in His wings.
Mild He lays His glory by,
Born that man no more may die,
Born to raise the sons of earth,
Born to give them second birth.
 Hark! the herald-angels sing
 Glory to the new-born King. Amen.

" Let us now go even unto Bethlehem."

31. O COME, all ye faithful,
  Joyfully triumphant;
O come ye, O come ye, to Bethlehem;
  Come and behold Him
  Born, the King of Angels;
  O come, let us adore Him,
  O come, let us adore Him,
O come, let us adore Him, CHRIST the LORD.

  GOD of GOD,
  LIGHT of LIGHT,
Lo! He abhors not the Virgin's womb;
  Very GOD,
  Begotten, not created;
  O come, let us adore Him,
  O come, let us adore Him,
O come, let us adore Him, CHRIST the LORD.

  Yea, LORD, we greet Thee,
  Born this happy morning;
JESU, to Thee be glory given;
  WORD of the FATHER,
  Late in time appearing;
  O come, let us adore Him,
  O come, let us adore Him,
O come, let us adore Him, CHRIST the LORD.
        Amen.

" Behold I bring you glad tidings of great joy."

32. Christians, awake, salute the happy morn,
Whereon the Saviour of mankind was born;
Rise to adore the mystery of love,
Which hosts of angels chanted from above;
With them the joyful tidings first begun
Of God Incarnate and the Virgin's Son.

Then to the watchful shepherds it was told,
Who heard the angelic herald's voice: "Behold,
I bring good tidings of a Saviour's birth
To you and all the nations upon earth:
This day hath God fulfilled His promised word,
This day is born a Saviour, Christ the Lord."

He spake; and straightway the celestial choir
In hymns of joy, unknown before, conspire:
The praises of redeeming love they sang,
And heaven's whole orb with alleluias rang:
God's highest glory was their anthem still,
Peace upon earth, and unto men good will.

To Bethlehem straight th' enlightened shepherds ran,
To see the wonders God had wrought for man:
Then to their flocks, still praising God, return,
And their glad hearts with holy rapture burn:
To all the joyful tidings they proclaim,
The first apostles of the Saviour's Name.

Oh! may we keep and ponder in our mind
God's wondrous love in saving lost mankind;
Trace we the Babe, Who hath retrieved our loss,
From the poor manger to the bitter cross;
Tread in His steps, assisted by His grace,
Till man's first Heavenly state again takes place.

Then may we hope, the angelic hosts among,
To join, redeemed, a glad triumphant throng:
He that was born upon this joyful day
Around us all His glory shall display;
Saved by His love, incessant we shall sing
Eternal praise to Heaven's Almighty King.
       Amen.

"Unto us a Child is born."

33. A BABE in Bethlehem is born,
And Salem greets the happy morn :

He in a narrow crib doth lie
Whose kingdom hath no boundary.

The ox, the ass, with one accord,
Confess that Babe to be the LORD :

While crowned kings from Saba bring
Gold, incense, myrrh, their offering.

They entering there, that threshold o'er,
Salute the young Prince and adore :

He comes—like us in flesh and blood,
Not in our sin's similitude;

Man's race unto His love to take,
Like God, and like Himself to make.

Then, magnify the Lord and bless,
In this His birth-day happiness.

Glory to Thee, O Lord of might,
An Infant born of Virgin bright:

Thee, Holy Trinity, we laud,
And give all thanks and praise to God.
        Amen.

"God, who at sundry times and in divers manners spake in time past unto the fathers by the prophets, hath in these last days spoken unto us by His Son, whom He hath appointed heir of all things, by whom also He made the worlds."

34. From lands that see the sun arise,
  To earth's remotest boundaries,
  The Virgin-born to-day we sing,
  The Son of Mary, Christ the King.

  Blest Author of this earthly frame,
  To take a servant's form He came,
  That liberating flesh by flesh,
  Whom He had made might live afresh.

In that chaste parent's holy womb
Celestial grace hath found its home:
And she, as earthly bride unknown,
Yet calls that Offspring blest her own:

The mansion of the modest breast
Becomes a shrine where GOD shall rest:
The pure and undefiled one
Conceived in her womb The Son.

That Son, that Royal Son she bore,
Whom Gabriel's voice had told afore:
Whom, in His Mother yet conceal'd,
The Infant Baptist had reveal'd.

The manger and the straw He bore,
The cradle did He not abhor;
By milk in infant portions fed,
Who gives e'en fowls their daily bread.

The Heav'nly chorus fill'd the sky,
The Angels sang to GOD on high,
What time to shepherds, watching lone,
They made Creation's Shepherd known.

For this Thine Advent glory be,
O JESU, Virgin-born to Thee!
With Father and with Holy Ghost,
From men and from the Heav'nly Host.
      Amen.

S STEPHEN.

"And they stoned Stephen, calling upon God."

35. Rightful Prince of Martyrs thou,
Bind the crown about thy brow;
Fairer far than fading wreath,
Weave we this thy crown of death.

Like a gem each rugged stone,
Sparkling with thy life-blood shone;
Nor could stars more brightly shine,
Studded round thy head divine.

From thy forehead's gushing streams
Dart a thousand blending beams,
Till thy glowing countenance
Lightens to an angel's glance.

Thou, the first slain victim free
To Him, the Victim slain for thee;
Thou the first thy Lord to own,
Sharer of His thorny crown.

First to tread the pointed road
Through the deep red sea of blood;
Prince of Martyrs, thee behind
What a countless army wind!

Glory to the Father be,
Glory, Virgin-born, to Thee,
Glory to the Holy Ghost,
Prais'd by men and heavenly host.
       Amen.

S. JOHN EVANGELIST.

"The Disciple whom Jesus loved."

36. The life which God's Incarnate Word
    Lived here below with men,
Three blest Evangelists record,
    With heaven-inspired pen;

John penetrates on eagle wing
    The Father's dread abode;
And shows the mystery wherein
    The word subsists with God.

Pure Saint! upon his Saviour's breast
    Invited to recline,
'Twas there he drew, in moments blest,
    His knowledge all divine:

There, too, with that angelic love
    Did he his bosom fill,
Which once enkindled from above,
    Breathes in his pages still.

O, dear to Christ!—to thee upon
    His cross, of all bereft,
Thou Virgin soul! the Virgin Son
    His Virgin Mother left.

To Jesus, born of Virgin bright,
    Praise with the Father be;
Praise to the Spirit Paraclete,
    Through all eternity.

THE HOLY INNOCENTS.

"These were redeemed from among men, being the first-fruits unto GOD and the LAMB."

37. HAIL, flowerets in the martyr crown!
Whom Herod's rage so soon hath strewn,
As, on the threshold of the morn,
Fresh rosebuds by the whirlwind shorn.

Sweet lambs of CHRIST! unasked ye gave
Your lives for Him who came to save;
Smiling beneath the murderer's frown,
Ye sported with your martyr's crown.

O'er Bethlehem's coasts deep woe is spread,
And hearts are wrung, and joys are fled;
But ONE survives the carnage wild,
The Virgin-born, the Royal Child.

THEE, Virgin-born! for aye we praise,
And high Thy natal glory raise;
THEE, FATHER! SPIRIT! we adore,
Blest THREE in ONE for evermore. Amen.

"These are they which follow the Lamb whithersoever He goeth."

38. A HYMN for Martyrs sweetly sing;
For Innocents your praises bring;
Of whom in tears was earth bereaved,
Whom Heaven with songs of joy received:
Whose angels see the FATHER's Face
World without end, and hymn His grace,
And, while they praise their glorious King,
A hymn for Martyrs sweetly sing.

A voice from Ramah was there sent,
A voice of weeping and lament,
While Rachel mourned her children sore
Whom for the tyrant's sword she bore.
Triumphal in their glory now
Whom earthly sufferings could not bow;
For whom, by cruel torments rent,
A voice from Ramah was there sent.

Fear not, O little flock and blest,
The lion that your life oppressed:
To Heavenly pastures ever new
The Heavenly Shepherd leadeth you,
Who dwelling now on Sion's hill
The Lamb's own footsteps follow still,
By tyrant there no more distressed:
Fear not, O little flock and blest.   Amen.

And every tear is wiped away
By your dear FATHER's hands for aye:
Death hath no power to hurt you more;
Your own is life's eternal shore.
And all who, good seed bearing, weep,
In everlasting joy shall reap;
What time they shine in heavenly day,
And every tear is wiped away. Amen.

CIRCUMCISION.

"The Blood of Jesus Christ our Lord cleanseth us from all sin."

39. O! HAPPY day, when first was poured
The blood of our redeeming Lord!
O.! happy day, when first began
His sufferings borne for sinful man!

Just entered on this world of woe,
His blood already learned to flow:
His future death was thus expressed,
And thus His early love confessed.

From heaven descending, to fulfill
The mandates of His Father's will,
E'en now behold the Victim lie,
The lamb of God, prepared to die.

Beneath the knife behold the Child,
The Innocent, the Undefiled;
For captives He the ransom pays,
For lawless man the law obeys.

Lord! circumcise our hearts, we pray;
Our fleshly natures purge away;
Thy Name, Thy likeness, may they bear:
Yea, stamp Thy holy Image there!

The Father's Name we loudly raise;
The Son, the Virgin-born, we praise;
The Holy Ghost we all adore;
One God, both now and evermore!
Amen.

EPIPHANY.

"We have seen His Star in the East, and are come to worship Him."

40. BRIGHTEST and best of the sons of the morning!
    Dawn on our darkness, and lend us thine aid;
Star of the East, the horizon adorning,
    Guide where our Infant Redeemer is laid.

Cold on His cradle the dew-drops are shining,
    Low lies His bed with the beasts of the stall;
Angels adore Him in slumber reclining,
    Maker, and Monarch, and SAVIOUR of all.

Offer Him gifts then in costly devotion,
    Odours of Edom, and incense divine;
Gems of the mountain and pearls of the ocean,
    Myrrh from the forest, and gold from the mine.

Brightest and best of the sons of the morning!
   Dawn on our darkness, and lend us thine aid;
Star of the East, the horizon adorning,
   Guide where our Infant Redeemer is laid.
                           Amen.

"The Gentiles shall come to Thy light, and kings to the brightness of Thy rising."

41. What star is this, with beams so bright,
   A stranger midst the orbs of light?
   It shines to herald forth the King,
   Glad tidings of our God to bring.

   See now fulfilled what God decreed,
   "From Jacob shall a star proceed:"
   And lo! the Eastern sages stand,
   To read in Heaven the Lord's command.

   And soon within their hearts do shine
   Rays fairer still and more divine,
   Which summon them with force benign,
   To seek the Giver of the sign.

   True love can brook no dull delay,
   Through toils and dangers lies their way;
   And yet their home, their friends, their all,
   They leave at once, at God's high call.

Oh, while the star of heavenly grace
Invites us, LORD, to seek Thy Face,
May we no more that grace repel,
Or quench that light, which shines so well!

To GOD the FATHER, GOD the SON,
And HOLY SPIRIT, THREE in ONE,
May every tongue and nation raise
An endless song of thankful praise!
Amen.

PART I.
"His Name shall be called Jesus."

42. JESU! the very thought of Thee
    With sweetness fills my breast;
But sweeter far thy face to see,
    And in thy presence rest.

Nor voice can sing, nor heart can frame,
    Nor can the memory find,
A sweeter sound than thy blest name,
    O Saviour of mankind!

O hope of every contrite heart,
    O joy of all the meek,
To those who fall, how kind Thou art!
    How good to those who seek!

But what to those who find? ah! this
    Nor tongue nor pen can show:
The love of Jesus, what it is,
    None but his lov'd ones know.

Jesu ! our only joy be Thou,
    As Thou our prize wilt be ;
Jesu ! be Thou our glory now,
    And through eternity.

Part II.

O Jesu ! King most wonderful !
    Thou Conqueror renowned !
Thou Sweetness most ineffable !
    In whom all joys are found !

When once Thou visitest the heart,
    Then truth begins to shine ;
Then earthly vanities depart ;
    Then kindles love divine.

O Jesu ! Light of all below !
    Thou fount of life and fire !
Surpassing all the joys we know,
    All that we can desire :

May every heart confess thy name,
    And ever Thee adore ;
And seeking Thee, itself inflame
    To seek Thee more and more.

Thee may our tongues for ever bless ;
    Thee may we love alone ;
And ever in our lives express
    The image of thine own.

Part III.

O Jesu ! Thou the beauty art
  Of angel worlds above ;
Thy Name is music to the heart,
  Enchanting it with love.

Celestial sweetness unalloy'd !
  Who eat Thee hunger still ;
Who drink of Thee still feel a void,
  Which nought but Thou can fill.

O my sweet Jesu ! hear the sighs
  Which unto Thee I send ;
To Thee mine inmost spirit cries,
  My being's hope and end !

Stay with us, Lord, and with thy light
  Illume the soul's abyss ;
Scatter the darkness of our night,
  And fill the world with bliss.

O Jesu ! spotless Virgin flower !
  Our life and joy ! to Thee
Be praise, beatitude, and power,
  Through all eternity. Amen.

"And He went down with them, and came to Nazareth, and was subject unto them."

43. In stature grows the Heavenly CHILD
   With death before His eyes,
  A LAMB unblemished, meek and mild,
   Prepared for Sacrifice.

  The SON of GOD His glory hides
   With parents mean and poor,
  And He, Who made the heavens, abides
   In dwelling-place obscure.

  Those mighty Hands, that rule the sky,
   No earthly toil refuse,
  And He, Who sets the stars on high,
   An humble path pursues.

  He, Whom as their ALMIGHTY LORD
   The angels swift obey,
  Now to an earthly parent's word
   Doth meek obedience pay.

  The FATHER's Name we loudly raise,
   The SON we all adore,
  The HOLY GHOST, One GOD, we praise,
   Both now and evermore.   Amen.

"And Jesus went about all the cities and villages, teaching in their synagogues, and preaching the Gospel of the Kingdom, and healing every sickness and every disease among the people."

44. Through Judah's land the Saviour walks,
    The word of life to teach;
His own He seeks—His own refuse
    To hearken to His speech.

And yet the miracles He works
    The Son of God proclaim;
The deaf can hear, the dumb pronounce
    The great Messiah's Name.

But no! they turn their hearts away,
    His doctrine they repel;
They hate the Sun, because they love
    Their night of sin too well.

But we, O God, Thy light desire,
    That shines so bright, so fair;
O guard our hearts, that there may be
    No love of darkness there!

O ever on Thy chosen saints
    Such blessings, Lord, bestow!
O may Thy truth for ever shine,
    Thy love for ever glow!

To God the Father, God the Son,
    And God the Holy Ghost,
Be glory from the saints on earth,
    And from the heavenly host. Amen.

"I heard a great voice of much people in Heaven saying, Alleluia."

45. ALLELUIA ! best and sweetest
    Of the hymns of praise above !
Alleluia ! thou repeatest,
    Angel-host, these notes of love.
        This ye utter,
While your golden harps ye move.

Alleluia ! Church victorious,
    Join the concert of the sky !
Alleluia ! bright and glorious,
    Lift, ye saints, this strain on high !
        We, poor exiles,
Join not yet your melody.

Alleluia ! strains of gladness
    Suit not souls with anguish torn :
Alleluia ! sounds of sadness
    Best become our state forlorn :
        Our offences
We with bitter tears must mourn.

But our earnest supplication,
    Holy God ! we raise to Thee :
Visit us with Thy salvation,
    Make us all Thy joys to see :
        Alleluia !
Ours at length this strain shall be.
                      Amen.

"Thy sun shall no more go down; neither shall Thy moon withdraw itself; for the LORD shall be thine everlasting light, and the days of Thy mourning shall be ended."

46. CHRIST, Whose glory fills the skies;
CHRIST, the true, the only Light,
Sun of Righteousness, arise,
Triumph o'er the shades of night;
Day-spring from on high, draw near;
Day-star, in our hearts appear.

Dark and cheerless is the morn,
LORD, if it be reft of Thee;
Joyless is the day's return,
Till Thy mercy's beams we see,
Till they pour their gladdening light
Through the darkness of our night.

Visit then these souls of Thine,
Pierce the gloom of sin and grief;
Fill us, LORD, with light divine;
Scatter all our unbelief;
More and more Thyself display,
Shining to the perfect day.

FATHER, glory be to Thee,
Glory to the Blessed SON,
Glory to the SPIRIT be,
Glory to the THREE in ONE;
As it was, is now, shall be,
Filling all eternity.   Amen.

"And Thou Bethlehem in the land of Judah art not the least among the cities of Judah."

47. BETHLEHEM! of noblest cities,
　　Nothing can with thee compare;
Thou alone the Lord from Heaven
　　Didst for us Incarnate bear.

Fairer than the sun at morning
　　Was the star that told His birth;
To the lands their God announcing,
　　Hid beneath a form of earth.

By its lambent beauty guided,
　　See, the Eastern Kings appear;
See them bend their gifts to offer—
　　Gifts of incense, gold, and myrrh.

Offerings of mystic meaning!—
　　Incense doth the God disclose;
Gold a royal child proclaimeth;
　　Myrrh a future tomb foreshows.

Holy Jesu! in Thy brightness
　　To the Gentile world display'd!
With the Father, and the Spirit,
　　Endless praise to Thee be paid.
　　　　　　　　　　　Amen.

SEPTUAGESIMA.

"As in Adam all die, so in Chirst shall all be made alive."

48. SEE from on high, array'd in truth and grace,
　　The FATHER's Word descend!
Burning to heal the wounds of Adam's race,
　　And our long evils end! Amen.

Pitying the miseries which with the Fall
 In Paradise began,
Prostrate upon the earth, the Lord of all
 Entreats for ruin'd man.

Oh, bitter then was our Redeemer's lot,
 While whelm'd in griefs unknown:
"Father," He cries, "remove this cup; yet not
 My will, but Thine be done."

While, a dread anguish pressing down his heart,
 He faints upon the ground;
And from each bursting pore the blood-drops start,
 Moistening the earth around.

But quickly, from high Heav'n, an angel came,
 To soothe the Saviour's woes;
And, strength returning to his languid frame,
 Up from the earth He rose.

Praise to the Father; praise, O Son! to Thee,
 To Whom a name is given
Above all names; Praise to the Spirit be,
 From all in earth and Heaven. Amen.

"I come to do Thy will O God."

49. Daughter of Sion! cease thy bitter tears,
   And calm thy breast;
Foretold through ages past, lo! now appears
   Thy Mediator blest.

That garden, where of old our guilt began,
   Wrought death and pain;
But this, where Jesus prays by night for man,
   Brings life and joy again.

Hither, of His own will, the Lord, for all
   Comes to atone;
And stays the thunderbolts about to fall
   From the dread Father's throne.

So shall He break the adamantine chain
   Of Hell's abyss;
And opening Heav'n long clos'd, call us again
   To His eternal bliss.

Praise to the Son, to whom a name above
   All name is given;
Praise to the Father and the Spirit of love,
   From all in earth and Heaven. Amen.

SEXAGESIMA.

50. Thou, Creator, art possess'd
   Of unbroken endless rest,
   Choirs angelic sing to Thee
   With unceasing melody.

We who lost fair Eden's bowers,
Shame and painful toil are ours;
Mourning exiles, how shall they
Sing their distant country's lay?

Thou who never dost despise
Bleeding hearts and weeping eyes,
Teach us our offence to know,
Bid the tears of sorrow flow.

Blessed tears that bring relief,
Faith and hope assuaging grief,
Peace the broken heart regains,
Sweetly flow the joyful strains.

God the Father, God the Son,
God the Spirit, Three in One,
Honour, glory, love, and praise,
Be to Thee through endless days.

QUINQUAGESIMA.

"These all died in faith, not having received the promises, but having seen them afar off, and were persuaded of them, and embraced them, and confessed that they were strangers and pilgrims on the earth."

51. O YE who followed CHRIST in love,
While yet He dwelt in realms above,
First children of Almighty grace,
First fathers of the faithful race,

Who can, in words of equal worth,
The wonders of your faith set forth;
Or tell of all the longing sighs
Of hope, uplifted to the skies?

Strangers and pilgrims here below
Ye deemed the world an empty show;
To purer joys your hearts were given,
The resting-place ye sought was Heaven.

The soul that truly cleaves to GOD,
Still longs to gain that blest abode;
SAVIOUR, forbid our souls to roam,
And fix them on our future home.

To GOD the FATHER, God the SON,
And GOD the SPIRIT, THREE in ONE,
Eternal praise to Each be given,
By all on earth and all in Heaven.
       Amen.

HYMNS.

PART II.

LENT.

" Turn ye even unto Me with all your heart, and with fasting, and with weeping, and with mourning."

52. Once more the solemn season calls
    A holy fast to keep ;
And now within the sacred walls
    Let priest and people weep.

But come not thou with tears alone,
    Or outward form of prayer ;
But let it in thy heart be known,
    That penitence is there.

Thy breast to beat, thy clothes to rend,
    God asketh not of thee ;
Thy stubborn soul He bids the bend
    In true humility.

O let us then with heartfelt grief,
  Draw near unto our God,
And pray to Him to grant relief,
  And stay th' uplifted rod.

O Righteous Judge, if Thou wilt deign
  Thine anger to relent,
Then grant us time to turn again
  In sorrow penitent.

Blest Three in One, with grief sincere,
  To Thee we humbly pray,
In fruits of love and holy fear
  To bless this fasting day.   Amen.

"Be ye therefore followers of God, as dear children; And walk in love, as Christ also hath loved us, and hath given himself for us an offering and a sacrifice to God for a sweet smelling savour.

53. Lo! now is our accepted day,
  The med'cine purging sin away;
  Where'er our lives have wrought offence,
  By thought and word, by deed and sense!

For God, the merciful and true,
  Hath spar'd his people hitherto;
  Nor us and ours, with searching eyes,
  Destroy'd for our iniquities.

Him therefore now, with earnest care,
And contrite fast, and tear and pray'r,
And works of mercy and of love,
We pray for pardon from above:

That from pollution making whole,
With virtues He may deck each soul,
And join us, in the Heav'nly place,
To Angel cohorts by His grace.

O Father, that we ask be done,
Through Jesus Christ, Thine Only Son;
Who, with the Holy Ghost and Thee,
Shall live and reign eternally. Amen.

"We then, as workers together with him, beseech you also that you receive not the grace of God in vain. For he saith, I have heard thee in a time accepted, and in the day of salvation have I succoured thee."

54. O Maker of the World, give ear!
Accept the pray'r, and own the tear,
Toward Thy seat of mercy sent
In this most holy fast of Lent.

Each heart is manifest to Thee:
Thou knowest our infirmity:
Forgive Thou then each soul that fain
Would seek to Thee, and turn again.

Our sins are manifold and sore;
But pardon them that sin deplore:
And for Thy Name's sake, make each
 soul
That feels and owns its languor whole.

So mortify we ev'ry sense,
By grace of outward abstinence,
That from each stain and spot of sin
The soul may keep her fast within.

Grant, O Thou Blessed Trinity,
Grant, O Essential Unity,
That this our fast of forty days
May work our profit, and Thy praise.
Amen.

"For this ye know, that no whoremonger, nor unclean person, nor covetous man, who is an idolater, hath any inheritance in the kingdom of Christ and of God."

55. Jesu, the Law and Pattern, whence
 Our forty days of abstinence,
 Who souls to save, that else had died,
 This sacred fast hast ratified:

 That so to Paradise once more,
 Might abstinence preserv'd restore
 Them that had lost its fields of light,
 Through crafty wiles of appetite:

Be present now, be present here,
And mark Thy Church's falling tear,
And own the grief that fills her eyes
In mourning her iniquities.

Oh, by Thy Grace be pardon won,
For sins that former years have done;
And let Thy mercy guard us still
From crimes that threaten future ill.

That by the Fast we offer here,
Our annual sacrifice sincere,
To Paschal gladness at the end,
Set free from guilt, our souls may tend.

O Father, that we ask be done,
Through Jesus Christ, Thine Only Son,
Who, with the Holy Ghost and Thee,
Shall live and reign eternally.   Amen.

"Surely, he hath borne our griefs, and carried our sorrows."

56. Saviour, when in dust to Thee
Low we bow th' adoring knee;
When, repentant, to the skies
Scarce we lift our weeping eyes,
O by all Thy pains and woe
Suffered once for man below,
Bending from Thy Throne on high
Hear our solemn litany!

By Thy helpless infant years,
By Thy life of want and tears,
By Thy fasting and distress
In the lonely wilderness,
By the dread mysterious hour
Of th' insulting tempter's power,
Turn, O turn a favouring eye,
Hear our solemn litany!

By Thy prayer thrice heard on high,
By Thine hour of Agony,
By the Cross, the Nail, the Thorn,
Piercing Spear, and torturing scorn,
By the gloom that veiled the skies
O'er the dreadful Sacrifice,
Listen to our humble cry,
Hear our solemn litany!

By Thy deep expiring groan,
By the sealed sepulchral stone,
By Thy triumph o'er the grave,
By Thy power from death to save—
O from earth to Heaven restored,
Mighty re-ascended Lord!
Prince and Saviour, heed our cry,
Hear our solemn litany! Amen.

"One of the soldiers with a spear pierced His side, and forthwith came thereout blood and water."

57. Rock of Ages! cleft for me,
    Let me hide myself in Thee;
    Let the water and the blood,
    From Thy wounded side which flow'd,
    Be of sin the double cure;
    Save from wrath, and make me pure.

    Merit I have none to bring,
    Only to Thy Cross I cling:
    Should my tears for ever flow,
    Should my zeal no languor know,
    All for sin could not atone;
    Thou must save, and Thou alone.

    While I draw this fleeting breath,
    When mine eyelids close in death,
    When I rise to worlds unknown,
    See Thee on Thy judgment throne,
    Rock of Ages! cleft for me,
    Let me hide myself in Thee.   Amen.

"A broken and contrite heart, O God, Thou wilt not despise."

58. Lord, when we bend before Thy throne,
    And our confessions pour,
  Teach us to hate the sins we own,
    And shun what we deplore.

Our humble spirits pitying see ;
　True penitence impart ;
And let a healing ray from Thee
　Beam hope on every heart.

When we disclose our wants in prayer,
　May we our wills resign ;
And not a wish our bosoms share,
　Which is not wholly Thine.

In meek submission to Thy will
　Let every prayer arise ;
And teach us, Lord, 'tis goodness still,
　That grants it, or denies.

To praise the Father and the Son,
　And Spirit, all divine,
The One in Three, and Three in One,
　Let saints and angels join.　Amen.

" God forbid that I should glory save in the Cross of our Lord Jesus Christ, by Whom the world is crucified unto me, and I unto the world."

59.　When I survey the wondrous Cross,
　　　On which the Prince of Glory died,
　　My richest gain I count but loss,
　　　And pour contempt on all my pride.

Forbid it, Lord, that I should boast,
  Save in the death of Christ my God :
All the vain things that charm me most
  I sacrifice them to His Blood.

See from His head, His hands, His feet,
  Sorrow and love flow mingling down !
Did e'er such love and sorrow meet,
  Or thorns compose so rich a crown ?

Were the whole realm of nature mine,
  That were an offering far too small ;
Love so amazing, so divine,
  Demands my life, my soul, my all.
                                        Amen.

PASSION TIDE.

[The 5th Sunday in Lent is called Passion Sunday.]

"Christ being come an high-priest of good things to come, by a greater and more perfect tabernacle, not made with hands, that is to say, not of this building ; neither by the blood of goats and calves, but by his own blood he entered in once into the holy place, having obtained eternal redemption for us."

60. The Royal Banners forward go :
    The Cross shines forth in mystic glow ;
    Where He in flesh, our flesh Who made,
    Our sentence bore, our ransom paid.

Where deep for us the spear was dy'd,
Life's torrent rushing from His side,
To wash us in that precious flood
Where mingled Water flow'd, and Blood.

Fulfill'd is all that David told
In true Prophetic song of old ;
Amidst the nations, God, saith he,
Hath reign'd and triumph'd from the Tree.

O Tree of beauty, Tree of light !
O Tree with royal purple dight !
Elect on whose triumphal breast
Those holy limbs should find their rest :

On whose dear arms, so widely flung,
The weight of this world's ransom hung;
The price of human kind to pay,
And spoil the Spoiler of his prey.

To Thee, Eternal Three in One,
Let homage meet by all be done :
Whom by the Cross thou dost restore,
Preserve and govern evermore ! Amen.

"Christ being come an high-priest of good things to come, by a greater and more perfect tabernacle, not made with hands, that is to say, not of this building; neither by the blood of goats and calves, but by his own blood he entered in once into the holy place, having obtained eternal redemption for us."

61. Sing, my tongue, the glorious battle,
    With completed victory rife:
And above the Cross's trophy
    Tell the triumph of the strife:
How the world's Redeemer conquer'd
    By surrend'ring of His life.

God, His Maker, sorely grieving
    That the first-made Adam fell,
When he ate the fruit of sorrow,
    Whose reward was death and hell,
Noted then this wood, the ruin
    Of the ancient wood to quell.

For the work of our salvation
    Needs would have his order so;
And the multiform deceiver's
    Art by art would overthrow;
And from thence would bring the med'cine
    Whence the insult of the foe.

Wherefore when the sacred fullness
    Of th' appointed time was come,
This world's Maker left His Father,
    Sent the Heavenly mansion from,
And proceeded, God Incarnate,
    Of the Virgin's Holy Womb

To the Trinity be be glory
  Everlasting, as is meet ;
Equal to the Father, equal
  To the Son and Paraclete ;
Trinal Unity, Whose praises
  All created things repeat.   Amen.

" Let this mind be in you, which was also in Christ
Jesus : Who, being in the form of God, thought it not
robbery to be equal with God : But made himself of no
reputation, and took upon him the form of a servant,
and was made in the likeness of men."

62. Thirty years among us dwelling,
      His appointed time fulfill'd,
    Born for this, He meets His Passion,
      For that this he freely will'd ;
    On the Cross the Lamb is lifted,
      Where His life-blood shall be spill'd.

    He endur'd the nails, the spitting,
      Vinegar, and spear, and reed ;
    From that holy Body Broken
      Blood and water forth proceed :
    Earth and stars, and sky, and ocean,
      By that flood from stain are freed.

Faithful Cross! above all other,
  One and only noble Tree!
None in foliage, none in blossom,
  None in fruit thy peers may be!
Sweetest wood and sweetest iron,
  Sweetest weight is hung on thee!

Bend thy boughs, O Tree of glory!
  Thy relaxing sinews bend!
And awhile the ancient rigour,
  That thy birth bestow'd, suspend:
And the King of Heavenly beauty
  On thy bosom gently tend.

Thou alone wert counted worthy
  This world's ransom to uphold:
For the shipwreck'd world preparing
  Harbour like the Ark of old;
With the Sacred Blood anointed,
  From the smitten Lamb that roll'd.

To the Trinity be glory
  Everlasting, as is meet;
Equal to the Father, equal
  To the Son and Paraclete;
Trinal Unity, Whose praises
  All created things repeat. Amen.

PALM SUNDAY AND HOLY WEEK.

"Tell ye the daughter of Sion, behold Thy King cometh unto thee, meek, and sitting upon an ass, and a colt, the foal of an ass."

63. Ride on ! ride on in majesty !
　　Hark ! all the tribes, Hosanna cry ;
　　O Saviour meek, pursue Thy road,
　　With palms and scattered garments strewed.

　　Ride on ! ride on in majesty !
　　In lowly pomp, ride on to die !
　　O Christ, Thy triumphs now begin
　　O'er captive death and conquered sin.

　　Ride on ! ride on in majesty !
　　The Angel armies of the sky
　　Look down with sad and wondering eyes
　　To see the approaching Sacrifice.

　　Ride on ! ride on in majesty !
　　The last and fiercest strife is nigh :
　　The Father on His sapphire Throne
　　Expects His Own anointed Son.

　　Ride on ! ride on in majesty !
　　In lowly pomp ride on to die !
　　Bow Thy meek Head to mortal pain,
　　Then take, O God, Thy Power, and reign.

Reign on! reign on in majesty!
Reign on in triumph, Lord most High!
We hymn Thee on Thy Throne of love,
Almighty King, in realms above.   Amen.

"And Abraham took the wood of the burnt-offering, and laid it upon Isaac his son."

"And they took Jesus, and led Him away. And He, bearing His Cross, went forth into a place called the place of a skull, which is called in the Hebrew Golgotha, where they crucified Him."

64. His trial o'er and now beneath
    His own Cross faintly bending,
Jesus, true Isaac, to His death
    Is wearily ascending.

And now, His hands and feet pierced thro'
    Upon the Cross they raise Him,
Where even now, in distant view,
    The eye of faith surveys Him.

O wondrous love, which God, most high,
    Toward man was pleased to cherish!
His sinless Son He gave to die,
    That sinners might not perish.

Our sin's pollution to remove,
    His Blood was asked and given,
So mighty was the Saviour's love,
    So vast the wrath of heaven.

Yes! 'tis the Cross that breaks the rod
   And chain of condemnation,
And makes a league 'twixt man and God,
   For our entire salvation.

O praise the Father, praise the Son,
   The Lamb for sinners given,
And Holy Ghost, through Whom alone
   Our hearts are raised to Heaven.
                          Amen.

"It is finished."

65. See the destined day arise;
    See, a willing sacrifice,
    Jesus, to redeem our loss,
    Hangs upon the shameful Cross.

    Jesu! who but Thou had borne,
    Lifted on that tree of scorn,
    Every pang and bitter throe,
    Finishing Thy life of woe?

    Who but Thou had dared to drain,
    Steeped in gall, the Cup of pain;
    And with tender body bear
    Thorns, and Nails, and piercing Spear?

    Thence the cleansing Water flowed,
    Mingled from Thy Side with Blood;
    Sign to all attesting eyes
    Of the finish'd sacrifice.

Holy Jesu ! grant us grace
In that Sacrifice to place
All our trust for life renew'd,
Pardoned sin, and promised good.
                              Amen.

*When this hymn is sung on Good Friday, the following
       words may be introduced between each verse.*

"Is it nothing to you, all ye that pass by ?
Behold, and see if there be any sorrow like
unto My sorrow."

"Now there stood by the Cross of Jesus His Mother."

67. By the Cross, sad vigil keeping,
    Stood the Mother doleful, weeping,
       Where her Son extended hung :
    For her soul, of joy bereaved,
    Smit with anguish, deeply grieved,
       Lo ! the piercing sword had wrung.

    O, how sad and sore distressed
    Now was she, that Mother blessed
       Of the Sole-begotten One !
    Woe-begone, with heart's prostration,
    Mother meek, the bitter Passion
       Saw she of her glorious Son.

Who, on Christ's fond Mother looking,
Such extreme affliction brooking,
  Born of woman, would not weep?
Who, on Christ's fond mother thinking,
Such a cup of sorrow drinking,
  Would not share her sorrows deep?

For His people's sins rejected,
She her Jesus unprotected
  Saw with thorns, with scourges rent:
Saw her Son from judgment taken,
Her Beloved in death forsaken,
  Till His spirit forth He sent.

With Thy Mother's deep devotion
Make me feel her strong emotion,
  Fount of love, Redeemer kind;
That my heart, fresh ardour proving,
Thee my God and Saviour loving,
  May with Thee acceptance find!
                            Amen.

EASTER EVE.

"Thou shalt not leave My Soul in hell, neither shalt Thou suffer Thy Holy One to see corruption."

67. All is o'er, the pain, the sorrow,
  Human taunts and Satan's spite;
Death shall be despoiled to-morrow
  Of the prey he grasps to-night;
Yet once more, to seal his doom,
Christ must sleep within the tomb.

Fierce and deadly was the anguish,
  Which on yonder Cross He bore ;
How did soul and body languish,
  Till the toil of death was o'er ;
But that toil, so fierce and dread,
Bruised and crushed the Serpent's head.

Close and still the cell that holds Him,
  While in brief repose He lies ;
Deep the slumber that enfolds Him,
  Veiled awhile from mortal eyes :
Slumber such as needs must be
After hard-won victory.

All night long with plaintive voicing
  Chant His requiem soft and low ;
Loftier strains of loud rejoicing
  From to-morrow's harp shall flow ;
"Death and Hell at length are slain,
Christ hath triumphed, Christ doth reign."
                                      Amen.

EASTER DAY.

"The Lord is risen."

68. Jesus Christ is risen to-day,   Alleluia !
    Our triumphant holy day,   Alleluia !
    Who did once upon the Cross,   Alleluia !
    Suffer to redeem our loss,   Alleluia !

Hymns of praise then let us sing, Alleluia !
Unto Christ our Heavenly King, Alleluia !
Who endured the Cross and grave, Alleluia!
Sinners to redeem and save, Alleluia !

But the pain which He endured, Alleluia !
Man's salvation hath procured, Alleluia !
Now above the sky He's King, Alleluia !
Where the Angels ever sing, Alleluia !
           Amen.

"O death where is thy sting? O grave where is thy victory?

69. Ye Choirs of New Jerusalem,
  To sweet new strains attune your theme!
  The while we keep, from care releas'd,
  With sober joy our Paschal Feast.

  When Christ, unconquer'd Lion, first
  The Dragon's chains by rising burst:
  And while with living voice He cries,
  The dead of other ages rise.

  Engorg'd in former years, their prey
  Must Death and Hell restore to-day:
  And many a captive soul, set free,
  With Jesus leaves captivity.

Right gloriously He triumphs now,
Worthy to Whom should all things bow:
And joining Heav'n and earth again
Links in one common-weal the twain.

And we, as these His deeds we sing,
His suppliant soldiers, pray our King,
That in His Palace, bright and vast,
We may keep watch and ward at last.

Long as unending ages run,
To God the Father laud be done:
To God the Son our equal praise,
And God the Holy Ghost, we raise.
       Amen.

EASTER TIDE.

"You hath he quickened together with him, having forgiven you all trespasses; Blotting out the handwriting of ordinances that was against us, which was contrary to us, and took it out of the way, nailing it to his cross; and having spoiled principalities and powers, he made a shew of them openly, triumphing in it."

70. Light's glitt'ring morn bedecks the sky,
Heav'n thunders forth its victor cry;
The glad earth shouts its triumphs high,
And groaning Hell makes wild reply.

While He, the King of glories might,
Treads down death's strength in death's despite,
And trampling Hell by victor's right,
Brings forth His sleeping saints to light.

Fast barr'd beneath the stone of late,
In watch and ward where soldiers wait,
Now shining in triumphant state,
He rises victor from death's gate.

Hell's pains are loos'd, and tears are fled;
Captivity is captive led;
The Angel, crown'd with light, hath said,
"The Lord is risen from the dead."

Th' Apostles' hearts were full of pain,
For their dear Lord so lately slain,
That Lord His servants' wicked train,
With bitter scorn had dared arraign.

We pray Thee, King with glory deck'd,
In this our Paschal joy, protect
From all that death would fain effect,
Thy ransom'd flock, Thine own elect.

To Thee Who, dead, again dost live,
All glory, Lord, Thy people give:
All glory, as is ever meet,
To Father and to Paraclete.   Amen.

"And the angel answered and said unto the women, Fear not ye; for I know that ye seek Jesus, which was crucified. He is not here; for he is risen as he said."

71. With gentle voice the Angel gave
The Women tidings at the grave;
Forthwith your Master shall ye see;
He goes before to Galilee.

And while with fear and joy they press'd
To tell these tidings to the rest,
Their Lord, their living Lord, they meet,
And see His Form, and kiss His Feet.

Th' Eleven when they hear, with speed
To Galilee forthwith proceed;
That there they may behold once more
The Lord's dear Face, as oft afore.

In this our bright and Paschal day
The sun shines out with purer ray:
When Christ, to earthly sight made plain,
The glad Apostles see again.

The wounds, the riven wounds he shows,
In that His Flesh with light that glows,
With public voice both far and nigh
The Lord's arising testify.

O Christ, the King, who lov'st to bless,
Do Thou our hearts and souls possess;
To Thee our praise that we may pay,
To Whom our laud is due, for aye.

We pray Thee, King with glory deck'd,
In this our Paschal joy, protect
From all that death would fain effect,
Thy ransom'd flock, Thine own elect.

To Thee, who dead again dost live,
All glory, Lord, Thy people give :
All glory, as is ever meet,
To Father and to Paraclete.   Amen.

"Christ being raised from the dead, dieth no more."

72. To the Paschal Victim,
Christians, bring the sacrifice of praise.

The Lamb the sheep hath ransom'd ;
Christ the undefiled, sinners to His God and
    Father hath recoucil'd.

Death and life, in wondrous strife, came to
    conflict sharp and sore ;
Life's Monarch, He that died, now dies no
    more.

What thou sawest, Mary, say,
As thou wentest on the way ?

I saw the Slain One's earthly prison :
I saw the glory of the Risen :—

The witness-Angels by the cave :
And the garments of the grave.

The Lord, my Hope hath risen ;
And he shall go before to Galilee.

We know that Christ is risen from death indeed :—
Thou victor Monarch, for Thy suppliants plead. Amen. Alleluia !

"If we believe that Jesus died and rose again, even so them also which sleep in Jesus will God bring with him."

73. Jesu lives ! no longer now
    Can thy terrors, Death, appal us :
Jesu lives ! and this we know,
    Thou, O Grave, canst not enthral us.
               Alleluia !

Jesu lives ! to Him the throne
    Over all the world is given :
His will go where He is gone,
    Rest and reign with Him in Heaven.
                Alleluia !

Jesu lives ! for us He died :
    Then alone to Jesu living
Pure in heart may we abide,
    Glory to our Saviour giving.
                Alleluia !

Jesu lives! we know full well
  Nought from us His love shall sever
Life, nor death, nor powers of hell
  Tear us from His keeping ever.
                    Alleluia!

Jesu lives! henceforth is death
  But the gate of life immortal;
This shall calm our trembling breath
  When we pass its gloomy portal.
                    Alleluia!

———

"He hath led captivity captive."

74. The foe behind, the deep before,
  Our hosts have dared and passed the sea:
And Pharaoh's warriors strew the shore,
  And Israel's ransomed tribes are free.

Lift up, lift up your voices now!
  The whole wide world rejoices now;
The Lord hath triumphed gloriously:
  The Lord shall reign victoriously!

Happy morrow, turning sorrow
  Into peace and mirth!
Bondage ending, love descending
  O'er the earth!
Seals assuring, guards securing,
  Watch His earthly prison:
Seals are shattered, guards are scattered,
  Christ hath risen.

No longer must the mourners weep,
  Nor call departed Christians dead ;
For death is hallowed into sleep,
  And every grave becomes a bed.

Now once more Eden's door
  Open stands to mortal eyes :
For Christ hath risen,
  And man shall rise.
Now at last, all things past,
  Hope and joy and peace begin :
For Christ hath won,
  And man shall win.

It is not exile, rest on high :
  It is not sadness, peace from strife :
To fall asleep is not to die :
  To dwell with Christ is better life.

Where our banner leads us, we may safely go :
Where our Chief precedes us we may face the foe :
His right arm is o'er us, He our guide will be ;
Christ hath gone before us; Christians follow ye !

He shall soon deliver from every woe,
                      Alleluia,
  If His paths ye tread;
Pleasures, as a river, shall round you flow,
                      Alleluia !
When ye see your Head.

With loins up-girt, and staff in hand,
  And hasty mien, and sandaled feet,
Around the Paschal Feast we stand,
  And of the Paschal Lamb we eat.

So shall He collect us, direct us, protect us,
    From Egypt's strand;
So shall He precede us, and feed us, and lead us
    To Canaan's land.

Toils and foes assailing, friends quailing, hearts failing,
    Shall threat in vain :
If He be providing, presiding, and guiding
    To Him again.

Christ our Leader, Monarch, Pleader, Interceder,
    Praise we and adore;
Exultation, veneration, gratulation,
    Bringing evermore.

Once despised, and once rejected,
Was this stone ; that now elected,
To a Corner-stone perfected,
As a glorious trophy stands erected.
                              Amen.

"Whom God hath raised up, having loosed the pains of death; because it was not possible he should be holden of it."

75. Jesu, Who brought'st Redemption nigh,
Word of the Father, God most high :
O Light of Light, to man unknown,
And watchful Guardian of Thine own :

Thy Hand Creation made and guides ;
Thy Wisdom time from time divides ;
By this world's cares and toils oppress'd,
O give our weary bodies rest.

That while in frames of sin and pain,
A little longer we remain,
Our flesh may here in such wise sleep,
That watch with Christ our souls may keep.

O free us, while we dwell below,
From insults of our ghostly foe,
That he may ne'er victorious be
O'er them that are redeem'd by Thee.

We pray Thee, King with Glory deck'd,
In this our Paschal joy, protect,
From all that Death would fain effect,
Thy ransom'd flock, Thine Own elect.

To Thee Who, dead, again dost live,
All glory, Lord, Thy people give ;
All glory, as is ever meet,
To Father, and to Paraclete.   Amen.

ASCENSION.

"The former treatise have I made, O Theophilus, of all that Jesus began both to do and teach, until the day in which he was taken up, after that he through the Holy Ghost had given commandments unto the apostles whom he had chosen."

76. Eternal Monarch, King most High,
Whose Blood hath brought Redemption nigh,
By Whom the death of Death was wrought,
And conqu'ring Grace's battle fought.

Ascending to the Throne of might,
And seated at the Father's right,
All pow'r in Heav'n is Jesu's Own,
That here His manhood had not known.

That so, in Nature's triple frame,
Each heav'nly and each earthly name,
And things in Hell's abyss abhorr'd,
May bend the knee and own Him Lord.

Yea, angels tremble when they see
How chang'd is our humanity,
That flesh hath purg'd what flesh had stain'd,
And God, the Flesh of God, hath reign'd.

Be Thou our Joy and Thou our Guard,
Who art to be our great Reward:
Our glory and our boast in Thee
For ever and for ever be!

All glory, Lord, to Thee we pay,
Ascending o'er the stars to-day;
All glory, as is ever meet,
To Father and to Paraclete. Amen.

"So then after the Lord had spoken unto them, he was received up into heaven, and sat on the right hand of God."

77. Jesu, Redemption all divine,
Whom here we love, for Whom we pine,
God, working out Creation's plan,
And, in the latter time, made Man:

What love of Thine was that, which led
To take our woes upon Thy head,
And pangs and cruel death to bear,
To ransom us from death's despair!

To Thee Hell's gate gave ready way,
Demanding there his captive prey:
And now in pomp and victor's pride,
Thou sittest at the Father's side.

Let very mercy force Thee still
To spare us, conqu'ring all our ill;
And, granting that we ask, on high
With Thine Own Face to satisfy.

Be Thou our Joy, and Thou our Guard,
Who art to be our great Reward:
Our glory and our boast in Thee
For ever and for ever be!

All glory, Lord, to Thee we pay,
Ascending o'er the stars to-day ;
All glory, as is ever meet,
To Father, and to Paraclete. Amen.

"Lift up your heads, O ye gates, be ye lift up, ye everlasting doors, and the King of Glory shall come in."

78. Hail! the day that sees Him rise, Alleluia.
Glorious to His native skies, Alleluia.
Christ, awhile to mortals given, Alleluia.
Enters now the highest Heaven. Alleluia.

Thee the glorious triumph waits, Alleluia.
Lift your heads, eternal gates ! Alleluia.
Christ has vanquish'd death and sin, Alleluia.
Take the King of Glory in, Alleluia.

Lo ! the Heav'n its Lord receives, Alleluia.
Yet He loves the earth He leaves : Alleluia.
Though returning to His Throne, Alleluia.
Still He calls mankind His own. Alleluia.

Still for us He intercedes, Alleluia.
His prevailing Death He pleads, Alleluia.
Near Himself prepares our place, Alleluia.
Harbinger of human race. Alleluia.

O though parted from our sight, Alleluia.
Far above the azure height, Alleluia.
Grant our hearts may thither rise, Alleluia.
Seeking Thee above the skies. Alleluia.
                               Amen.

" A cloud received Him out of their sight."

79. Blest Saviour, now, Thy work is done !
Death owns Thy power, the prize is won !
Triumphant now we see Thee rise,
Returning to Thy native skies.

A radiant cloud is now Thy seat,
And earth lies stretched beneath Thy Feet ;
Ten thousand thousand angels sing,
To welcome their returning King.

Beside the everlasting gates,
The Angel-host enraptured waits,
His throne receives the eternal Son,
Both God and Man for ever One.

There, Jesu, Thou hast never ceased
To be our Friend, our great High Priest.
Pleading in our behalf Thy Blood,
That holy, reconciling flood ;

And thence the Church, Thy chosen Bride,
With spiritual gifts supplied,
Through all her members draws from Thee,
Her hidden life of sanctity.

All praise from every heart and tongue,
To our Ascended Lord be sung ;
The Father's praise let all confess,
And all the Holy Spirit bless.   Amen.

"I go to prepare a place for you."

80. O Christ ! Who hast prepared a place
For us around Thy throne of grace,
We pray Thee, lift our hearts above,
And draw them with the cords of love !

Source of all good, Thou, gracious Lord !
Art our exceeding great reward ;
How transient is our present pain !
How boundless our eternal gain !

With open face and joyful heart,
We then shall see Thee as Thou art ;
Our love shall never cease to glow,
Our praise shall never cease to flow.

Thy never-failing grace to prove,
A surety of Thine endless love,
Send down Thy Holy Ghost to be
The raiser of our souls to Thee.

O future Judge ! Eternal Lord !
Thy Name be hallowed and adored :
To God the Father, King of Heaven,
And Holy Ghost, like praise be given.
       Amen.

"Through His mercy He saved us."

O Christ! our Hope, our hearts' Desire,
   Redemption's only spring!
Creator of the world art Thou,
   Its Saviour and its King.

How vast the mercy and the love
   Which laid our sins on Thee,
And led Thee to a cruel death,
   To set Thy people free!

But now the bonds of death are burst,
   The Ransom has been paid;
And Thou art on Thy Father's Throne,
   In glorious robes arrayed.

O may Thy mighty love prevail,
   Our sinful souls to spare!
O may we come before Thy Throne,
   And find acceptance there!

O Christ! be Thou our present joy,
   Our future great Reward!
Our only glory may it be,
   To glory in the Lord! Amen.

WHITSUNDAY.

"And it came to pass, while he blessed them, he was parted from them and carried up into heaven."

82. Blest joys for mighty wonders wrought
The year's revolving orb has brought,
What time the Holy Ghost in flame
Upon the Lord's disciples came.

The quiv'ring fire their heads bedew'd,
In cloven tongues' similitude,
That eloquent their words might be,
And fervid all their charity.

In varying tongues the Lord they praised,
The gath'ring nations stood amazed:
And whom the Comforter Divine
Inspir'd, they mock'd as full of wine.

These things were done in type to-day,
When Eastertide had worn away
The number told, which once set free
The captive at the Jubilee.

Thy servants, falling on their face,
Beseech Thy mercy, God of Grace,
To send us, from Thy heav'nly Seat,
The blessings of the Paraclete.

To God the Father, God the Son,
And God the Spirit, praise be done :
And Christ the Saviour on us send
The Spirit's Gift, world without end.
                              Amen.

"And when the day of Pentecost was fully come, they were all with one accord in one place. And suddenly there came a sound from heaven as of a rushing mighty wind, and it filled the house where they were sitting."—

83. Come, Holy Ghost, our souls inspire,
And lighten with celestial fire:
Thou the anointing Spirit art,
Who dost Thy sev'n-fold gifts impart.

Thy blessed Unction from above,
Is comfort, life, and fire of love:
Enable with perpetual light
The dullness of our blinded sight.

Anoint and cheer our soiled face
With the abundance of Thy grace:
Keep far our foes, give peace at home;
Where Thou art Guide no ill can come.

Teach us to know the Father, Son,
And Thee, of Both, to be but One:
That through the ages all along,
This may be our endless song;
Praise to Thy eternal merit,
Father, Son, and Holy Spirit.   Amen.

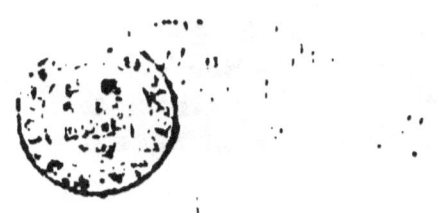

"They spake with other tongues as the Spirit gave them utterance."

84. Again the slowly circling year
    Brings round the blessed hour,
When on the Saints the Comforter
    Came down with grace and power.

In fashion of a fiery tongue
    The mighty Godhead came;
Their lips with eloquence He strung,
    And fill'd their hearts with flame.

Straightway with divers tongues they speak,
    Instinct with grace divine;
While wondering crowds the cause mistake,
    And deem them drunk with wine.

God of all grace! to Thee we pray,
    To Thee adoring bend;
Into our hearts this sacred day
    Thy Spirit's fullness send.

Thou who in ages past didst pour
    Thy graces from above,—
Thy grace in us where lost restore,
    And 'stablish peace and love.

All glory to the Father be;
    And to the Son Who rose;
Glory, O Holy Ghost, to Thee,
    While age on ages flows. Amen.

"*The Comforter Whom I will send unto you.*"

85. Holy Spirit! Lord of Light!
From Thy clear celestial height,
 Thy pure beaming radiance give.
Come, Thou Father of the poor!
Come with treasures which endure!
 Come, Thou light of all that live!

Thou, of all Consolers best,
Visiting the troubled breast,
 Dost refreshing peace bestow;
Thou in toil art comfort sweet;
Pleasant coolness in the heat;
 Solace in the midst of woe.

Light immortal! light divine!
Visit Thou these hearts of Thine,
 And our inmost being fill:
If Thou take Thy grace away,
Nothing pure in man will stay;
 All his good is turn'd to ill.

Heal our wounds, our strength renew;
On our dryness pour Thy dew;
 Wash the stains of guilt away;
Bend the stubborn heart and will;
Melt the frozen, warm the chill;
 Guide the steps that go astray.

Thou, on those who evermore
Thee confess, and Thee adore,
In Thy seven-fold gifts descend;
Give them comfort when they die;
Give them life with Thee on high;
Give them joys which never end.
                                Amen.

TRINITY.

"The grace of our Lord Jesus Christ, and the love of God, and the communion of the Holy Ghost, be with you all. Amen."

86. Be present, Holy Trinity:
Like splendour, and One Deity:
Of things above, and things below,
Beginning that no end shall know.

Thee all the armies of the sky
Adore, and laud, and magnify:
And Nature, in her triple frame,
For ever sanctifies Thy name.

And we, too, thanks and homage pay,
Thine own adoring flock to-day:
O join to that celestial song
The praises of our suppliant throng!

Light, sole and one, we Thee confess,
With triple praise we rightly bless;
Alpha and Omega we own,
With ev'ry spirit round Thy Throne.

To Thee, O Unbegotten One,
And Thee, O Sole begotten Son :
And Thee, O Holy Ghost, we raise
Our equal and eternal praise.   Amen.

"There are Three that bare record in Heaven."

87. Thrice Holy God, of wondrous might,
　　O Trinity of love divine,
To Thee belongs unclouded light,
　　And everlasting joys are Thine.

About Thy Throne dark clouds abound,
　　About Thee shine such dazzling rays,
That Angels as they stand around
　　Are fain to tremble as they gaze.

Thy new-born people, gracious Lord,
　　Confess Thee in Thine own great Name ;
By hope they taste the rich reward,
　　Which faith already dares to claim.

Father, may we Thy law fulfill,
　　Blest Son, may we Thy precepts learn,
And Thou, Blest Spirit, guide our will,
　　Our feet unto Thy pathway turn.

Yea, Father, may Thy will be done,
　　And may we thus Thy Name adore,
Together with Thy blessed Son,
　　And Holy Ghost, for evermore.   Amen.

"Holy! Holy! Holy!"

88. O Thou, Who dwellest bright on high,
Thou ever-blessed Trinity!
Thee we confess, in Thee believe,
To Thee with pious heart we cleave.

O Father! by Thy saints adored,
O Son of God! our Blessed Lord,
O Holy Spirit! Who dost join
Father and Son with love divine.

We see the Father in the Son,
And with the Father, Christ is One;
The Holy Ghost, the Paraclete,
In Both resides, in Both complete.

For God the Father, God the Son,
And God the Holy Ghost are One;
All Three one blessed truth approve,
All Three compose one holy love.

To God the Father, God the Son,
And Holy Ghost, be glory done;
One God Almighty we adore,
With heart and voice, for evermore!
       Amen.

"Holy! Holy! Holy!"

89. Holy, holy, holy! Lord God Almighty!
Early in the morning our song shall rise to Thee,
Holy, holy, holy! merciful and mighty!
God in Three Persons, blessed Trinity!

Holy, holy, holy! all the saints adore Thee,
Casting down their golden crowns around the glassy sea;
Cherubim and seraphim falling down before Thee,
Which wert, and art, and evermore shalt be.

Holy, holy, holy! though the darkness hide Thee,
Though the eye of sinful man Thy glory may not see,
Only Thou art holy: there is none beside Thee
Perfect in power, in love and purity!

Holy, holy, holy! Lord God Almighty
All Thy works shall praise Thy name, in earth, and sky, and sea!
Holy, holy, holy! merciful and mighty!
God in Three Persons, blessed Trinity!
        Amen.

"Blessing, and glory, and wisdom, and thanksgiving, and honour, and power, and might, be unto our God for ever and ever. Amen."

90. Father of all, to Thee we raise
The tribute of our grateful praise,
Who for our twofold life hast given
Bread from the earth, and Bread from heaven.

Thou too, O Jesus, be adored,
The only Son, the Almighty Lord;
Who, our Salvation to become,
Didst not abhor the Virgin's womb!

Who, on the Cross a Victim made,
The ransom of the world hast paid;
Through Whom alone on guilty men
The hope of life has dawned again.

And Thou, by Whose Almighty aid
A Virgin pure, a holy Maid
Brought forth Incarnate Deity,
Eternal Spirit, praise to Thee!

Three Persons, but One God, Whose grace
Both forms and saves our human race,
With joyful hearts and lips to Thee
We hymn this mighty Mystery.

To God the Father, with the Son,
And Holy Spirit, Three in One,
Laud, honour, glory, majesty
Now, and henceforth for ever be.   Amen.

TRINITY SUNDAY.

"There are Three that bare record in Heaven, the Father, the Word, and the Holy Ghost; and these Three are One."

91. Thou ever blessed Trinity!
Dwelling in Light, a Mystery!
Thee we confess, in Thee believe,
To Thee with pious heart we cleave.

O Father, by Thy Saints adored!
O Son of God, the Christ, the Lord!
O Holy Spirit! Who dost join
Father and Son with Love Divine!

We know the Father in the Son;
That with the Father Christ is One;
The Holy Ghost, the Paraclete,
With Both is one, in Both complete.

Thou God the Father, God the Son,
And God the Holy Ghost are One;
One perfect Truth in Trinity,
One Holy Love in Unity.

To God the Father, God the Son,
And Holy Ghost, in glory One;
The Lord Almighty we adore
With heart and voice for evermore.
      Amen.

HYMNS.

PART III.

COMMEMORATION OF APOSTLES.

"Verily their sound went into all the earth; their words unto the ends of the world."

92 Th' Eternal gifts of Christ the King,
    The Apostles' glorious deeds we sing;
    Their hard-won palms and circling rays
    Demand our joyous hymns of praise.

    Princes of all the Churches they,
    Crowned chieftains of th' unearthly fray,
    Of Heaven's high courts the warriors bright,
    For ever set the world's true light.

    Theirs is the Saints' unwavering Faith,
    The Hope that triumphs over death,
    The Love of Christ in perfect glow,
    That laid the world's fell tyrant low.

In them the FATHER's glory bright,
In them the SON's triumphant might,
In them abides the SPIRIT's will;
They the wide Heaven with gladness fill.

To GOD the FATHER, and the SON,
And Thee, Blest SPIRIT, THREE in ONE;
As aye it was, and aye shall be,
All praise through all Eternity.   Amen.

"Their sound went into all the earth, and their words unto the ends of the world."

23.   DISPOSER Supreme,
    And Judge of the earth,
Who choosest for Thine
    The weak and the poor;
To frail earthern vessels
    And things of no worth
Entrusting Thy riches
    Which aye shall endure;

Those vessels soon fail,
    Though full of Thy light,
And at Thy decree
    Are broken and gone;
Thence brightly appeareth
    Thy truth in its might,
As through the clouds riven
    The lightnings have shone.

Like clouds are they borne
  To do Thy great will,
And swift as the winds
  About the world go;
The WORD with His wisdom
  Their spirits doth fill,
They thunder, they lighten,
  The waters o'erflow.

Their sound goeth forth,
  "CHRIST JESUS the LORD;"
Then Satan doth fear,
  His citadels fall:
As when the dread trumpets
  Went forth at Thy word,
And one long blast shattered
  The Canaanite's wall.

O loud be their trump,
  And stirring their sound
To rouse us, O LORD,
  From slumber of sin;
The lights Thou hast kindled
  In darkness around,
Oh, may they illumine
  Our spirits within.

All honour and praise,
  Dominion, and might,
To GOD THREE in ONE
  Eternally be,
    2F

Who round us hath shed
His marvellous light,
And called us from darkness
His glory to see. Amen.

"And they went forth, and preached everywhere the Lord working with them, and confirming the word with signs following."

94 Let all on earth with songs rejoice,
Let Heaven return th' exulting voice,
Let Heaven and earth together raise
The great Apostles' glorious praise.

Thou, at Whose word they spread the light
Of Heav'nly Truth o'er heathen night,
Lights of the world for evermore,
Their light, O Lord, around us pour.

Thou, at Whose will to them 'twas given
To bind or loose in earth and Heaven,
Our chains unbind, our sins remove,
And lift our souls to things above.

Thou, in Whose might they spake the word,
Which cured disease and health restored,
To us its healing power prolong,
Support the weak, confirm the strong.

And when Thou, LORD, again shalt come
To speak the world's unerring doom,
Oh! then with them pronounce us blest,
And place us in Thine endless rest.

To Thee, O FATHER! SON, to Thee!
To Thee, Blest SPIRIT! glory be;
As ever was in ages past,
And shall be still while ages last. Amen.

COMMEMORATION OF EVANGELISTS.

"How beautiful upon the mountains are the feet of him that bringeth good tidings, that publisheth peace."

95   HERALDS of CHRIST! through whom go forth
Glad tidings o'er th' awakening earth,
Unfolding the mysterious plan
Of Love Divine to sinful man.

The mysteries, which beneath the law
The prophets in dim shadows saw,
Did ye behold in open day,
When former shadows passed away.

The woes which GOD as Man hath borne,
The works which Man as GOD hath done;
All this ye wrote as GOD decreed,
That ages yet unborn might read.

Though far removed in time and space,
One SPIRIT guides you by His Grace:
In you that SPIRIT still is given
To guide us in the way of Heaven.
        Amen.

COMMEMORATION OF MARTYRS.

"All my delight is upon the Saints, that are in the earth: and upon such as excel in virtue."

96. BLESSED Feasts of Blessed Martyrs!
 Saintly days of saintly men!
With affection's recollections
 Greet we your return again.

 Mighty deeds they wrought, and wonders,
  While a frame of flesh they bore:
 We with meetest praise, and sweetest,
  Honour them for evermore.

Faith unflinching, Hope unquenching,
  Well-loved Lord, and single heart,—
Thus they glorious and victorious,
  Bore the Martyr's happy part.

Blood in slaughter pour'd like water,
  Torment's long and heavy chain,
Flame, and axe, and laceration,
  They endured, and conquered pain.

While they pass'd through divers tortures,
  Till they sank by death oppress'd,
Earth's rejected were elected,
  To have portion with the Blest.

By contempt of worldly pleasures,
  And by mighty battles done,
They have reach'd the land of Angels,
  And with them are knit in one.

They are made co-heirs of glory,
  And they sit with Christ on high :
Oh' that, as He heard their weeping,
  He might also hear our cry.

Till, this weary life completed,
  And its many labours past,
He shall grant us to be seated
  In our Father's Home at last !
                    Amen.

"These are they which came out of great tribulation, and have washed their robes and made them white in the Blood of the Lamb."

97   O Thou of all Thy warriors, Lord,
 The Portion, Crown, and sure Reward!
 From sinful fetters set us free,
 Who sing Thy Martyr's victory.

 In selfish pleasures' worldly round
 The taste of bitter gall he found ;
 Sin's soft enticing lures disdained,
 And so the Heavenly Crown He gained.

 He bravely ran the painful race,
 Enduring with a hero's grace ;
 Thee with his blood on earth confessed,
 With Thee in Heaven for aye is blessed.

 We pray before Thee, bending low,
 All-pitying Lord, Thy Love to show ;
 On this Thy Martyr's triumph-day
 Our shame and guilt put far away.

 Now to the Father and the Son
 Be glory while all ages run :
 The same, O Holy Ghost, to Thee
 Through ages of Eternity.   Amen.

COMMEMORATION OF CONFESSORS.

And when the chief Shepherd shall appear, ye shall receive a Crown of glory that fadeth not away.

98   JESU, the world's Redeemer, hear !
Thy Bishop's fadeless crown, draw near !
Accept with gentler love to-day
The prayers and praises that we pay !

The day that crown'd with deathless fame
This meek Confessor of Thy Name,
Whose yearly feast, in solemn state,
Thy faithful people celebrate.

The world, and all its boasted good,
As vain and passing, he eschew'd ;
And therefore, with Angelic bands,
In endless joys for ever stands.

Grant then that we, O gracious God,
May follow in the steps he trod ;
And freed from ev'ry stain of sin,
As he hath won, may also win.

To Thee, O CHRIST, our loving King,
All glory, praise, and thanks we bring :
All glory, as is ever meet,
To Father and to Paraclete.   Amen.

COMMEMORATION OF VIRGINS.

"He that glorieth, let him glory in the Lord."

99   Jesu, the Virgins' Crown, do Thou
Accept us, as in pray'r we bow ;.
Born of that Virgin, whom alone
The Mother and the Maid we own.

Amongst the lilies Thou dost feed,
With Virgin choirs accompanied ;
With glory deck'd, the spotless brides
Whose bridal gifts Thy love provides.

They, wheresoe'er Thy footsteps bend
With hymns and praises still attend ;
For Thee they pour their sweetest song,
And after Thee rejoicing throng.

We pray Thee therefore to bestow
Upon our senses here below
Thy grace, that so we may endure
From taint of all corruption pure.

All laud to God the Father be;
All laud, Eternal Son, to Thee :
All laud, as is forever meet,
To God the Holy Paraclete.   Amen.

THE CONVERSION OF S. PAUL.

"Saul, Saul, why persecutest thou Me?"

100 'Gainst what foemen art thou rushing?
    Saul, what madness drives thee on?
Innocents in fury crushing,
    Children of the sinless One:
        O, how shortly
Shall He make His vengeance known!

See the LORD, from Heaven descending,
    Smites him, blinds him, lays him low;
See the persecutor bending
    Humbly, meekly, to the blow:
        See him rising,
Friend to CHRIST, no longer foe.

Breathing slaughter, chains preparing,
    O, how fierce his anger burned;
Trembling now, and lost his daring,
    Meek obedience he has learned;
        The destroyer
Now into a lamb is turned.

CHRIST, Thy power is man's salvation,
    Hardest hearts Thou mak'st Thine own;
He who wrought such desolation,
    That Thy Name might be o'erthrown,
        Now converted
Thro' the world that Name makes known.

Praise the FATHER, GOD of Heaven,
 Him who reigns supreme on high;
Praise the SON for sinners given
 Both to suffer and to die;
 Praise the SPIRIT
Guiding us most lovingly.   Amen.

THE PURIFICATION OF S. MARY THE VIRGIN.
(Commonly called)
THE PRESENTATION OF CHRIST IN THE TEMPLE.

" The LORD Whom ye seek, shall suddenly come to His temple."

101   O SION, open wide thy gates,
 Let figures disappear,
A Priest and Victim both in one,
 The truth Himself, is here.

 No more the simple flock shall bleed:
 Behold the FATHER'S SON
Himself to His own Altar comes,
 For sinners to atone.

 Conscious of hidden Deity
 The lowly Virgin brings
Her new-born Babe, with two young
  'doves,'
 Her tender offerings.

The hoary Simeon sees at last
  His LORD so long desired,
And hails, with Anna, Israel's Hope,
  With sudden rapture fired.

But silent knelt the Mother blest
  Of the yet silent WORD,
And, pondering all things in her heart,
  With speechless praise adored.

All glory to the FATHER be,
  All glory to the SON,
All glory, HOLY GHOST, to Thee,
  While endless ages run. Amen.

THE ANNUNCIATION OF THE BLESSED VIRGIN MARY.

"Behold, a Virgin shall be with child, and shall bring forth a SON, and they shall call His Name EMMANUEL, which being interpreted is, GOD with us."

102 PRAISE we the LORD this day,
  This day so long foretold,
Whose promise shone with cheering ray
  On waiting saints of old.

124

The Prophet gave the sign
  For faithful men to read ;
A Virgin, born of David's line,
  Shall bear the promised Seed.

Ask not how this should be,
  But worship and adore ;
Like her, whom Heaven's majesty
  Came down to shadow o'er.

Meekly she bowed her head
  To hear the gracious word,
Mary, the pure and lowly maid,
  The favoured of the LORD.

Blessed shall be her name
  In all the Church on earth,
Through whom that wondrous mercy came,
  Th' INCARNATE SAVIOUR'S birth.

JESU, the Virgin's SON,
  We praise Thee and adore,
Who art with GOD the FATHER One
  And SPIRIT evermore. Amen.

"Blessed art thou among women."

103 VIRGIN BORN! we bow before Thee!
Blessed was the womb that bore Thee!
Mary, Mother meek and mild,
Blessed was she in her Child!

Blessed was the breast that fed Thee!
Blessed was the hand that led Thee!
Blessed was the parent's eye,
That watch'd Thy slumbering infancy!

Blessed she by all creation,
Who brought forth the world's Salvation!
Blessed they, for ever blest,
Who love Thee most, and serve Thee best!

Virgin-born, we bow before Thee!
Blessed was the womb that bore Thee!
Mary, Mother meek and mild,
Blessed was she in her Child.
      Amen.

NATIVITY OF S. JOHN THE BAPTIST.

" In those days came John the Baptist, preaching in the wilderness of Judea, and saying, Repent ye, for the Kingdom of Heaven is at hand."

104 Lo, from the desert homes,
  Where he hath sojourned long,
 The new Elias comes,
  In sternest wisdom strong;
  The voice that cries
   Of CHRIST from high,
  And judgment nigh
 From opening skies.

 Your GOD e'en now doth stand
  At Heaven's opening door;
 His fan is in His Hand,
  And He will purge His floor;
  The wheat He claims,
   And with Him stows;
  The chaff He throws
 To deathless flames.

 Ye haughty mountains, bow
  Your sky-aspiring heads;
 Ye valleys, hiding low,
  Lift up your gentle meads;
  Make His way plain
   Your King before;
  For evermore
 He comes to reign.

May thy dread voice around,
   Thou harbinger of light,
On our dull ears still sound,
   Lest here we sleep in night,
      Till judgment come,
         And on our path
         Shall burst the wrath,
      And endless doom.

To GOD the FATHER, SON,
   And SPIRIT ever Blest,
Eternal THREE in ONE,
   All worship be addrest;
      As heretofore
         It was, is now,
         And shall be so
      For evermore.   Amen.

S. MICHAEL AND ALL ANGELS.

"This is God's host."

105 THE mighty host on high,
   Their joys beyond compare,
Their glories in the sky,
   The deeds they bravely dare:
For these the Church to-day
Pours forth her joyous lay,
To Heav'n's great princes praise to pay.

These are the chieftains bright,
　　Viceroys of God's domain,
Unwearied in their might
　　The demons to restrain:
To quell th' infernal foe,
And work their rivals woe,
These heav'nly warriors haste below.

Captains of mighty race,
　　And noble champions, they
The evil spirits chase,
　　Undaunted in the fray:
They speed, in ranks array'd,
The upright soul to aid,
And crown him victor undismay'd.

What tongue can here declare,
　　Fancy or thought descry,
The joys Thou dost prepare
　　For these thine hosts on high?
Who, for the warfare deck'd,
Their earthly friends protect,
And in right paths to Heav'n direct.

To Thee, O Lord most high,
　　One in Three Persons still,
To pardon us we cry,
　　And to preserve from ill;
That, after perils sore,
Thy Name we may adore
With holy Angels evermore.　　Amen.

"Are they not all ministering spirits, sent forth to minister for them who shall be heirs of Salvation?"

106 They come, God's Messengers of love,
They come from realms of peace above,
From homes of never-fading light,
From blissful mansions ever bright.

They come to watch around us here,
To soothe our sorrow, calm our fear:
Ye heav'nly Guides, speed not away;
God willeth you with us to stay.

But chiefly at its journey's end
'Tis yours the spirit to befriend;
And whisper to the willing heart,
"O Christian soul, in peace depart."

Blest Jesu! Thou, Whose groans and tears
Have sanctified frail nature's fears,
When to the earth in sorrow weighed
Thou didst not scorn Thine Angels' aid,

An Angel guard to us supply,
When on the bed of death we lie;
And by Thine Own Almighty Power
O shield us in the last dread hour.

To God the Father, God the Son,
And God the Spirit, Three in One,
From all above, and all below
Let joyful praise unceasing flow. Amen.

ALL SAINTS.

" After this I beheld, and lo, a great multitude. which no man could number."

107 SPOUSE of CHRIST! for Him contending
 O'er each clime beneath the sun,
 Blend with prayers for help ascending,
 Notes of praise for triumphs won.

 As the Church to day rejoices,
 All her Saints in one to join,
 So from earth let all our voices,
 Rise in melody divine.

 Mary leads the sacred story;
 Mary with her Heav'nly Child;
 Sharer with Him now in glory,
 Maid and Mother undefil'd.

 Angels next, in due gradation
 Of their ninefold ministry,
 Hymn the FATHER of Creation,
 Maker of the stars on high.

 John, the hearld-voice sonorous,
 More than prophet own'd to be,
 Patriarchs, and Seers, in chorus
 Swell th' Angelic harmony.

Near to CHRIST th' Apostles seated,
    Trampling on the powers of hell,
By the promise now completed,
    Judge the tribes of Israel.

They who nobly died believing,
    Martyrs, purpled in their gore,
Crowns of life by death receiving,
    Rest in joy for evermore.

Who, the world and death defying,
    JESUS faithfully confessed,
Living on yet daily dying,
    Numbered now among the Blessed:

All are blest together, praising
    GOD's Eternal Majesty,
Thrice-repeated anthems raising
    To the All-holy Trinity.

So may we, with hearts devoted,
    Serve our GOD in holiness;
So may we, by GOD promoted,
    Share that Heaven which they posses!
                      Amen.

"The Lamb which is in the midst of the Throne shall feed them, and shall lead them unto living fountains of waters; and God shall wipe away all tears from their eyes."

108 Who are these, like stars appearing,
    These, before GOD's Throne who stand?
Each a golden crown is wearing:
    Who are all this glorious band?
        Alleluia! hark! they sing,
        Praising loud their Heavenly King.

Who are these in dazzling brightness,
    Cleansed from every sinful stain?
These, whose robes of purest whiteness
    Ever radiant shall remain,
        Still untouched by Time's rude hand—
        Whence come all this glorious band?

These are they who have contended
    For their SAVIOUR's honour long,
Wrestling on till life was ended,
    Following not the sinful throng:
        These, who well the fight sustained,
        Triumph by the LAMB have gained.

These are they whose hearts were riven,
    Sore with woe and anguish tried,
Who in prayer full oft have striven
    With the GOD they glorified:
        Now their painful conflict o'er,
        GOD has bid them weep no more.

These, th' ALMIGHTY contemplating,
  Here as Priests before Him stand,
Soul and body always waiting
  Day and night at His command;
    Now in GOD's most holy place
    Blest they stand before His Face.

THREE in ONE, let all adore Thee,
  Saints on earth and Saints in Heaven,
Every creature bow before Thee,
  Who hath all their being given;
    All Thy Glory shall confess,
    Perfected in holiness.   Amen.

"If we suffer, we shall also reign with Him."

109 IF there be that skills to reckon
    All the number of the Blest,
  He, perchance, can weigh the gladness
    Of the everlasting rest
  Which, their earthly warfare finish'd,
    They through suff'ring have possess'd.

  Through the vale of lamentation
    Happily and safely past,
  Now the years of their affliction
    In their mem'ry they re-cast,
  And the end of all perfection
    They can contemplate at last.

For they see their cruel Tempter
  Suff'ring torments evermore;
To the Saviour That redeem'd them
  Those redeem'd ones praises pour;
And the Monarch That rewards them
  Those rewarded Saints adore.

In a glass, through types and riddles,
  Dwelling here, we see alone;
When serenly, purely, clearly,
  We shall know as we are known;
Fixing our enlighten'd vision
  On the glory of the Throne.

Their the Trinty of Persons
  Unbeclouded shall we see!
There the Unity of Essence
  Shall reveal'd in glory be;
While we hail the Three-fold Godhead
  And the simple Unity.

Wherefore, man, take heart and courage
  Whatsoe'er thy present pain;
Such untold reward through suff'ring
  Thou may'st merit to attain;
And for ever in His Glory
  With the Light of Light to reign.

Laud and honour to the Father;
  Laud and honour to the Son;
Laud and honour to the Spirit;
  Ever Three and ever One:
Consubstantial, Coeternal,
  While unending ages run.   Amen.

LAYING THE FOUNDATION STONE OF A CHURCH.

"The glory of Lebanon shall come unto Thee, the fir tree, the pine tree, and the box together, to beautify the place of My sanctuary."

110 O Lord of Hosts, Whose glory fills
The bounds of the eternal hills,
And yet vouchsafes, in Christian lands,
To dwell in temples made with hands.

Grant that all we, who here to-day
Rejoicing this foundation lay,
May be in very deed Thine own,
Built on the precious Corner-stone.

Endue the creatures with Thy grace,
That shall adorn Thy dwelling-place;
The beauty of the oak and pine,
The gold and silver, make them Thine.

To Thee they all pertain; to Thee
The treasures of the earth and sea;
And when we bring them to Thy throne
We but present Thee with Thine own.

The heads that guide endue with skill;
The hands that work preserve from ill;
That we, who these foundations lay,
May raise the top-stone in its day.

Both now and ever, LORD, protect
The temple of Thine own elect ;
Be Thou in them, and they in Thee,
O ever-blessed TRINITY ! Amen.

FEAST OF THE DEDICATION OF A CHURCH.

"This is none other but the House of GOD, and this is the gate of Heaven."

111 O WORD of GOD above
Who fillest all in all,
Hallow this house with Thy sure love,
And bless our festival.

Here from the Font is poured
Grace on each guilty child ;
The blest anointing of the LORD
Brightens the once defiled.

Here CHRIST to faithful hearts
His Body gives for food ;
The LAMB of GOD Himself imparts
The Chalice of His Blood.

Here guilty souls that pine
May health and pardon win ;
The Judge acquits, and grace divine
Restores the dead in sin.

Yea, God enthroned on high
  Here also dwells to bless;
Here trains adoring souls that sigh
  His mansions to possess.

Against this holy home
  Rude tempests harmless beat,
And Satan's angels fiercely come
  But to endure defeat.

All might, all praise be Thine
  Father, co-equal Son,
And Spirit, bond of love divine,
  While endless ages run.   Amen.

"I saw the holy city, New Jerusalem, coming down from God, out of Heaven, prepared as a bride adorned for her husband."

112 Blessed city, heavenly Salem,
       Vision dear of peace and love,
     Who of living stones art builded
       In the height of Heaven above,
     And, with angel hosts encircled,
       As a bride to earth doth move;

From celestial realms descending,
  Bridal glory round thee shed,
Meet for Him Whose love espoused thee,
  To thy LORD shalt thou be led;
All thy streets, and all thy bulwarks,
  Of pure gold are fashioned.

Bright thy gates of pearl are shining,
  They are open evermore;
And by virtue of His merits
  Thither faithful souls do soar,
Who for CHRIST's dear Name in this world
  Pain and tribulation bore.

Many a blow and biting sculpture
  Polished well those stones elect,
In their places now compacted
  By the heavenly Architect,
Who therewith hath willed forever
  That His Palace should be decked.

Praise and honour to the FATHER,
  Praise and honour to the SON,
Praise and honour to the SPIRIT,
  Ever Three, and ever One,
One in might and one in glory,
  While eternal ages run. Amen.

"Behold I lay in Sion a Chief Corner-stone, elect, precious."

113 CHRIST is made the sure Foundation,
    CHRIST the Head and Corner stone,
Chosen of the LORD, and precious,
    Binding all the Church in one,
Holy Sion's help for ever,
    And her confidence alone.

All that dedicated City,
    Dearly loved of GOD on high,
In exultant jubilation
    Pours perpetual melody;
GOD the One in Three adoring
    In glad hymns eternally.

To this Temple, where we call Thee,
    Come, O LORD of Hosts, to-day:
With Thy wonted loving-kindness,
    Hear Thy servants, as they pray;
And Thy fullest benediction
    Shed within its walls alway.

Here vouchsafe to all Thy servants
    What they ask of Thee to gain,
What they gain from Thee for ever
    With the Blessed to retain,
And hereafter in Thy glory
    Evermore with Thee to reign.

Praise and honour to the FATHER,
  Praise and honour to the SON,
Praise and honour to the SPIRIT,
  Ever Three, and ever One,
One in might, and One in glory,
  While eternal ages run. Amen.

EMBER DAYS.

"And the things that thou hast heard of Me among many witnesses, the same commit thou to faithful men, who shall be able to teach others also."

114 CHRIST is gone up: yet ere he passed
  From earth in Heaven to reign,
He formed one Holy Church to last
  Till He should come again.

His twelve Apostles first He made
  His ministers of Grace;
And they their hands on others laid,
  To fill in turn their place.

So age by age, and year by year,
  His grace was handed on;
And still the Holy Church is here,
  Although her LORD is gone.

Let those find pardon, LORD! from Thee,
  Whose love to her is cold;
Bring wanderers in, and let there be
  One Shepherd and one Fold.

To GOD the FATHER, GOD the SON,
  And GOD the HOLY GHOST,
By man on earth be glory done,
  And by the heavenly Host. Amen.

"Let Thy priests be clothed with righteousness."

115 LORD, pour Thy SPIRIT from on high,
  And Thine ordained servants bless;
Graces and gifts to each supply,
  And clothe Thy priests with righteousness.

Within Thy temple when they stand,
  To teach the truth as taught by Thee,
SAVIOUR, like stars in Thy right hand
  Let all Thy Church's pastors be.

Wisdom, and zeal, and love impart,
  Firmness and meekness from above,
To bear Thy people in their heart,
  And love the souls whom Thou dost love:

To love, and pray, and never faint,
By day and night their guard to keep,
To warn the sinner, form the saint,
To feed Thy lambs, and tend Thy sheep.

So, when their work is finished here,
They may in hope their charge resign;
So, when their Master shall appear,
They may with crowns of glory shine.
       Amen.

ROGATION DAYS.

" Ask and it shall be given you."

116 T ILL its holy hours are past,
  Watch we in our three days' fast;
  He who came for man to die
  Is not yet gone up on high—
  While He still vouchsafes to say,
  Let us more devoutly pray.

  None but Thou, O LORD, can know
  What a debt to Thee we owe:
  We Thy gracious yoke have spurn'd,
  All Thy lessons have unlearn'd:
  For Thy tender mercy yet
  O forgive us all that debt.

Many foes are round about,
Foes within, and foes without.
In temptation Thou didst share,
Who did once our weakness bear:
By those trials we would plead,
Safely us through danger lead.

Lord, Thou canst, if so Thou wilt,
Heal our cares, and cleanse our guilt;
For the power is Thine to save,
And to ransom from the grave.
O be all our trust in Thee,
Undivided Trinity!   Amen.

HOLY MATRIMONY.

" This is a great mystery."

116 The voice that breathed o'er Eden,
    That earliest wedding day,
  The primal marriage blessing,
    It hath not passed away:

  Still in the pure espousal
    Of Christian man and maid
  The Holy Three are with us,
    The threefold grace is said.

For dower of blessed children,
   For love and faith's sweet sake,
For high mysterious union
   Which naught on earth may break.

Be present, awful FATHER,
   To give away this bride,
As Eve Thou gavest to Adam
   Out of his own pierced side;

Be present, SON of Mary,
   To join their loving hands,
As Thou didst bind two natures
   In Thine eternal bands;

Be present, Holiest SPIRIT,
   To bless them as they kneel,
As Thou for CHRIST, the Bridegroom,
   The heavenly spouse does seal.

O spread Thy pure wing o'er them,
   Let no ill power find place,
When onward to Thine Altar
   The hallowed path they trace,

To cast their crowns before Thee
   In perfect sacrifice,
Till to the home of gladness
   With CHRIST's own Bride they rise.
                Amen.

SCHOOL FESTIVALS.

"That signs and wonders may be done by the Name of Thy Holy Child Jesus."

117 Lord Jesus, God and Man,
   For love of men a Child,
The very God, yet born on earth
   Of Mary undefiled;

Lord Jesus, God and Man,
   In this our festal day
To Thee for precious gifts of grace
   Thy ransomed people pray.

We pray for childlike hearts,
   For gentle holy love,
For strength to do Thy will below
   As angels do above.

We pray for simple faith,
   For hope that never faints,
For true communion evermore
   With all Thy blessed Saints.

On friends around us here
   O let Thy blessing fall,
We pray for grace to love them well,
   But Thee beyond them all.

O joy to live for Thee!
O joy in Thee to die!
O very joy of joys to see
Thy Face eternally!

Lord Jesus, God and Man,
We praise Thee and adore,
Who art with God the Father One,
And Spirit, evermore. Amen.

"Out of the mouth of babes and sucklings Thou hast perfected praise."

118   God eternal, mighty King,
Unto Thee our praise we bring;
All the earth doth worship Thee,
We amid the throng would be;

Holy, Holy, Holy! cry
Angels round Thy throne on high:
Lord of all the heavenly powers,
Be the same loud anthem ours.

Glorified Apostles rise
Night and day continual praise;
Hast not Thou a mission too
For Thy children here to do?

With the Prophets' goodly line,
We in mystic bond combine;
For Thou hast to us revealed
Things that to the wise were sealed.

Martyrs, in a noble host,
Of the cross are heard to boast:
Oh, that we our cross may bear,
And a crown of glory wear.

God eternal, mighty King,
Unto Thee our praise we bring;
To the FATHER, and the SON,
And the SPIRIT, Three in One. Amen.

"JESUS increased in wisdom and stature, and in favour with God and man."

119 O HOLY LORD, content to dwell
In a poor home, a lowly Child,
With meek obedience noting well
Each bidding of Thy mother mild;

Lead every child that bears Thy name
To walk in Thy pure upright way,
To shun the paths of sin and shame,
And humbly, like Thyself, obey.

Let not this world's unhallowed glow
The fresh baptismal dew efface,
Nor blast of sin too roughly blow,
And quench the trembling flame of grace.

Gather Thy lambs within Thine arm,
And gently in Thy bosom bear,
Protect them still from hurt and harm,
And bid them rest for ever there.

So shall they, waiting here below,
Like Thee, their LORD, a little span,
In wisdom and in stature grow,
And favour both with GOD and man.
       Amen.

THE HOURS OF PRAYER.
"Seven times a day will I praise Thee."
AT LAUDS, 3 A. M.
"Early will I seek Thee."

120 THE winged herald of the day
Proclaims the morn's approaching ray:
And CHRIST, the LORD our souls excites,
And so to endless life invites.

Take up thy bed, to each He cries,
Who sick, or wrapped in slumber lies:
And chaste, and just, and sober stand,
And watch: My coming is at hand.

With earnest cry, with tearful care,
Call we the LORD to hear our prayer,
While supplication, pure and deep,
Forbids each chastened heart to sleep.

Do Thou, O CHRIST, our slumbers wake;
Do Thou the chains of darkness break;
Purge Thou our former sins away,
And in our souls new light display.

All laud to GOD the FATHER be;
All laud, Eternal SON, to Thee;
All laud, as is for ever meet,
To GOD the Holy PARACLETE.   Amen.

AT PRIME, 6 A. M.

"I laid me down and slept, and rose up again; for the Lord sustained me."

121 OUR limbs with tranquil sleep refreshed,
    Lightly from rest we spring;
FATHER supreme! to us be nigh,
    While to Thy praise we sing.

Thy love be first in every heart,
    Thy name on every tongue;
Whatever we this day may do,
    May it in Thee be done.

Cut off in us, Almighty LORD,
　All that may lead to shame;
So with pure hearts may we in bliss
　Thine endless praise proclaim.

To GOD the FATHER, GOD the SON,
　And GOD the HOLY GHOST,
All glory be from saints on earth,
　And from the angel-host.　Amen.

AT TERCE, 9 A. M.

"It is but the third hour of the day."

122　COME, Holy Ghost, with God the Son,
　And God the Father, ever One;
　Shed forth Thy grace within our breast,
　And dwell with us, a ready guest.

　By ev'ry pow'r, by heart and tongue,
　By act and deed, Thy praise be sung;
　Inflame with perfect love each sense,
　That others' souls may kindle thence.

　O Father, that we ask be done,
　Through Jesus Christ, Thine Only Son,
　Who, with the Holy Ghost and Thee,
　Shall live and reign eternally.　Amen.

AT SEXT, 12 NOON.

" At noon-day will I pray."

123 O GOD of truth, O Lord of might,
Who ord'rest time and change aright,
And send'st the early morning ray,
And light'st the glow of perfect day;

Extinguish Thou each sinful fire,
And banish every ill desire;
And while Thou keep'st the body whole,
Shed forth Thy peace upon the soul.

O FATHER, that we ask be done,
Through JESUS CHRIST, Thine Only Son;
Who, with the HOLY GHOST and Thee,
Shall live and reign eternally.   Amen.

AT NONE, 3 P. M.

" The hour of prayer being the ninth hour."

124 O GOD, Unchangeable and True,
Of all the life and power,
Dispensing light and silence through
Every successive hour:

Lord, brighten our declining day,
   That it may never wane;
Till death, when all things round decay,
   Brings back the morn again.

This grace, on Thy redeem'd confer,
   FATHER, co-equal SON,
And HOLY GHOST, the Comforter;
   Eternal Three in ONE.   Amen.

AT VESPERS, 6 P. M.,

"It is towards evening, and the day is far spent."

125 BEFORE the ending of the day,
   Creator of the world, we pray
   That with Thy wonted favour Thou
   Would'st be our Guard and Keeper now.

From all ill dreams defend our eyes,
From nightly fears and fantasies;
Tread under foot our ghostly foe,
That no pollution we may know.

O Father, that we ask be done,
Through Jesus Christ, Thine Only Son;
Who, with the Holy Ghost and Thee,
Shall live and reign eternally.   Amen.

AT COMPLINE, 9 A. M.

"Ye that by night stand in the house of the Lord."

126 O BLEST CREATOR of the light!
 Who didst the dawn from darkness bring,
And in its new-born glory bright,
 Didst bid the world with life to spring.

Who gently blending eve with morn,
 And morn with eve, did'st call them day;
Now night's dark shade is o'er us borne,
 O hear us, as to Thee we pray.

Let not our souls, by guilt depressed,
 Or vexed by thoughts impure and vain,
So lose the way to endless rest,
 Drawn down by sin to earth again.

Teach us to knock at Heaven's high door,
 Teach us the prize of life to win;
Teach us all evil to abhor,
 And purify ourselves within

FATHER of mercies! hear our cry;
 Hear us, O Sole-begotten Son!
Hear us, O HOLY GHOST most high!
 Now, and while endless ages run.
       Amen.

MONDAY.

"And God made the firmament, and divided the waters which were under the firmament from the waters which were above the firmament. And the evening and the morning were the second day."

127 Come, let us praise the name of God,
    Who on the second day
Spread out the firmament above,
    His glory to display.

Slow floating on the blue expanse
    The watery clouds we view,
Whence fruitful showers at His command
    The thirsty soil bedew.

How fair an image of the Grace
    His mercy doth impart,
Like morning dew or gentle rain,
    To gladden every heart.

And when the faithful soul drinks in
    Those showers with blessings rife,
A well of water springeth up
    To everlasting life.

O happy saints, on whom are poured
    Such treasures from above;
Lord, may they ne'er forgetful be,
    But render love for love.

To GOD, Who freely loved us first,
　All might, all glory, be;
To FATHER, SON, and HOLY GHOST,
　Through all eternity.　Amen.

TUESDAY.

"The evening and the morning were the third day."

128　GOD speaks the word, the floods obey,
　　And sink into their bed;
　Forth rising from the deep to-day
　　Earth shows her new-born head.

　CHRIST took our flesh, and was a man,
　　And cleansed the stain we bore;
　Through Him, in the Baptismal flood,
　　We rise to life once more.

　As Thou hast purged Thy people, LORD,
　　In the life-giving flood,
　Keep us from sinning, lest we lose
　　The cleansing of Thy blood.　Amen.

WEDNESDAY.

"Let there be light and there was light."

"Woe to that man by whom the Son of man is betrayed."

129 God as on this day made the lights,
   Sun, moon, and stars, for days and nights;
   Sun, moon, and stars, are stedfast still,
   To run their course and do His will.

   To do His will, Christ left His throne,
   To work our good and not His own:
   By wicked men to death betray'd,
   By men whom He Himself had made.

   O Saviour, blessed be Thy Name!
   Thine is the glory, ours the shame:
   By all the pains Thy love endured
   Let all our many sins be cured.   Amen.

THURSDAY.

"O ye whales and all that move in the waters bless ye the Lord."

"He was carried up into Heaven."

130 The deep a two-fold offering bore,
      Men's bodies to maintain,
   The birds that skim the liquid air,
      The fish that cleave the main.

But we, baptized and raised in CHRIST,
  To GOD an offering rise:
Our sojourn the Baptismal deep,
  Our converse in the skies.

Thou art gone up to GOD's right hand
  For us to intercede,
And daily for our many sins,
  Thy sacrifice to plead.

While here we wait for the below,
  Vouchsafed our Food to be:
Dwell in us now, that we may dwell
  For evermore in Thee. Amen.

FRIDAY.

"Let us make man in our image."

"He was found in fashion as a man."

131 O THOU, Who when the world had birth,
Mad'st Adam living man from earth,
Whose mercy on our sire bestow'd
The likeness of his Parent GOD;—

Who when mankind's most deadly foe
Had lured him unto guilt and woe,
A mortal shape, with kindly care,
In mercy didst vouchsafe to wear;—

Who for lost man didst meekly deign
To undergo the Cross of pain;
Thou Lamb of God to slaughter led,
Whose precious blood for us was shed;—

To Thee our thankful hymns we raise,
In mingled penitence and praise;
Pardon our sins, O Lord, we pray,
And wash them in Thy blood away.
Amen.

SATURDAY.

"And on the seventh day God ended His work which he had made."

132 Six days of labour now are past;
    Thou restest, Holy God;
And with approving Eye hast seen
    That all is very good.

Blest is the seventh morn of light,
    Hallowed for rest divine;
Yet, Lord, a new creation needs
    That mighty power of Thine.

Ten thousand voices praise Thy Name
    In earth and sea and sky;
But fallen man by sin has marred
    The blissful harmony.

Come, Lord, create his heart anew;
  His heart of stone remove:
Then hymns of praise again shall rise,
  The fruits of holy love.

Oh! for the songs that Thou wilt bless,
  Where heart and voice agree;
Oh! for the prayers that plead aright
  With Thy dread Majesty.

All praise to God, the Three in One,
  Who high in glory reigns;
Who by His Word hath all things made,
  And by His Word sustains. Amen.

GENERAL HYMNS.

133 All people that on earth do dwell
  Sing to the Lord with cheerful voice;
Him serve with fear, His praise forth tell,
Come ye before Him and rejoice.

The Lord, ye know, is God indeed;
Without our aid he did us make:
We are His flock, He doth us feed,
And for His sheep He doth us take.

O enter then His gates with praise,
Approach with joy His courts unto;
Paise, laud, and bless His name always,
For it is seemly so to do.

For why? the LORD our GOD is good,
His mercy is for ever sure;
His Truth at all times firmly stood,
And shall from age to age endure.

To FATHER, SON, and HOLY GHOST,
The GOD Whom heaven and earth adore,
From men and from the angel-host
Be praise and glory evermore.   Amen.

---

134 FATHER of heaven, Whose love profound
A ransom for our souls hath found,
Before Thy Throne we sinners bend,
To us Thy pardoning love extend.

Almighty SON, Incarnate Word,
Our PROPHET, PRIEST, REDEEMER, LORD,
Before Thy Throne we sinners bend,
To us Thy saving grace extend.

Eternal SPIRIT, by whose breath
The soul is raised from sin and death;
Before Thy Throne we sinners bend,
To us Thy quickening power extend.

Thrice Holy! FATHER, SPIRIT, SON;
Mysterious GODHEAD, THREE in ONE,
Before Thy Throne we sinners bend,
Grace, pardon, life, to all extend.   Amen.

135 Our blest Redeemer, ere He breathed
   His tender last farewell,
A Guide, a Comforter, bequeathed
   With us to dwell.

He came sweet influence to impart,
   A gracious, willing Guest,
While He can find one humble heart,
   Wherein to rest.

And His that gentle voice we hear,
   Soft as the breath of even,
That checks each thought, that calms each
     fear,
   And speaks of Heaven.

And every virtue we possess,
   And every conquest won,
And every thought of holiness,
   Are His alone.

Spirit of purity and grace,
   Our weakness, pitying, see:
O make our hearts Thy dwelling place,
   And worthier Thee.

O praise the Father; praise the Son,
   Blest Spirit, praise to Thee;
And praise to God, the Three in One,
   The One in Three. Amen.

136 Brief life is here our portion;
　　Brief sorrow, short-lived care;
　The life that knows no ending,
　　The tearless life, is *there*.

　O happy retribution !
　　Short toil, eternal rest :
　For mortals and for sinners
　　A mansion with the blest,

　And now we fight the battle,
　　But then shall wear the crown
　Of full and everlasting
　　And passionless renown;

　And now we watch and struggle,
　　And now we live in hope.
　And Sion in her anguish
　　With Babylon must cope;

　But He Whom now we trust in
　　Shall then be seen and known
　And they that know and see Him
　　Shall have him for their own.

　The morning shall awaken,
　　The shadows shall decay,
　And each true-hearted servant
　　Shall shine as doth the day:

　There God, our King and Portion,
　　In fullness of His grace,
　Shall we behold for ever,
　　And worship face to face.

Part II.

To thee, O dear, dear Country
  Mine eyes their vigils keep;
For very love beholding
  Thy happy name, they weep:

The mention of Thy glory
  Is unction to the breast,
And medicine in sickness,
  And love, and life, and rest.

O one, O only Mansion!
  O Paradise of Joy!
Where tears are ever banished,
  And smiles have no alloy;

Beside thy living waters
  All plants are, great and small;
The cedar of the forest,
  The hyssop of the wall:

Thine ageless walls are bonded
  With amethyst all unpriced;
Thy saints build up its fabric,
  The corner-stone is Christ.

Thou hast no shore, fair ocean!
  Thou hast no time bright day!
Dear fountain of refreshment
  To pilgrims far away!

Upon the Rock of Ages
  They raise thy holy tower,
Thine is the victor's laurel,
  And thine the golden dower.

And all thine endless leisure
  In sweetest accents sings
The ills that were thy merit,
  The joys that are thy King's.

Part III.

Jerusalem, the golden !
  With milk and honey blest,
Beneath thy contemplation
  Sink heart and voice opprest.

Thy joys, when I would sing them,
  My spirit fails and faints,
And vainly would it image
  Th' assembly of the Saints.

They stand, those halls of Sion,
  Conjubilant with song,
And bright with many an angel,
  And all the martyr throng.

The Prince is ever in them,
  The light is aye serene ;
The pastures of the blessed
  Are decked in glorious sheen :

There is the Throne of David,
  And there, from toil released,
The shout of them that triumph,
  The song of them that feast ;

And they beneath their Leader,
  Who conquer'd in the fight,
For ever and for ever
  Are clad in robes of white.

The following may be sung at the end of each Part.

O sweet and blessed country,
  The Home of God's elect!
O sweet and blessed country,
  That eager hearts expect!

Jesu, in mercy bring us
  To that dear land of rest;
Who art, with God the Father,
  And Spirit ever blest. Amen.

---

137 Oh, what if we are Christ's
  Is earthly shame or loss?
Bright shall the crown of glory be
  When we have borne the Cross.

Keen was the trial once,
  Bitter the cup of woe,
When martyred Saints baptized in blood,
  Christ's sufferings shared below:

Bright is their glory now,
  Boundless their joy above,
Where on the bosom of their God
  They rest in perfect love.

Lord, may that grace be ours,
Like them in faith to bear
All that of sorrow, grief, or pain
May be our portion here :

Enough if Thou at last
The word of blessing give,
And let us rest beneath Thy feet,
Where saints and angels live.

All glory, Lord, to Thee,
Whom heaven and earth adore;
To Father, Son, and Holy Ghost,
One God for evermore. Amen.

---

138 The strain upraise of joy and praise,
    Alleluia.
To the glory of their King,
Shall the ransomed people sing,   Alleluia.

And the choirs that dwell on high,
Shall re-echo through the sky,   Alleluia.

They in the rest of Paradise who dwell,
The blessed ones, with joy the chorus swell,
    Alleluia.
The planets beaming on their heavenly way,
The shining constellations join, and say,
    Alleluia.

Ye clouds that onward sweep,
Ye winds on pinions light,
Ye thunders, echoing loud and deep,
Ye lightnings, wildly bright,
In sweet consent unite your　　　Alleluia.

Ye floods and ocean billows,
Ye storms and winter snow,
Ye days of cloudless beauty,
Hoar frost and summer glow,
Ye groves that wave in spring
And glorious forests sing　　　Alleluia.

First let the birds, with painted plumage gay,
Exalt their great Creator's praise, and say
　　　　　　　　　　　　Alleluia.
Then let the beasts of earth, with varying strain,
Join in creation's hymn, and cry again,
　　　　　　　　　　　　Alleluia.

Here let the mountains thunder forth sonorous,　　　　　　　　　　Alleluia.
There let the valleys sing in gentler chorus,
　　　　　　　　　　　　Alleluia.

Thou jubilant abyss of ocean, cry　Alleluia.
Ye tracts of earth and continents reply,
　　　　　　　　　　　　Alleluia.

To God, Who all creation made,
The frequent hymn be duly paid;   Alleluia.

This is the strain, the eternal strain, the Lord
　　Almighty loves ;　　　　　　Alleluia.
This is the song, the heavenly song, that
　　Christ the King approves :　　Alleluia.

Wherefore we sing, both heart and voice
　　awaking,　　　　　　　　Alleluia.
And children's voices echo, answer making,
　　　　　　　　　　　　　　Alleluia.
Now from all men be out-poured
Alleluia to the Lord ;
With Alleluia evermore,
The Son and Spirit we adore.
Praise be done to the Three in One.
　　Alleluia !　Alleluia !　Alleluia !　Amen.

139　Conquering kings their titles take
　　From the foes they captive make;
　　Jesus, by a nobler deed,
　　From the thousands He hath freed.

　　　Yes; none other name is given
　　　Unto mortals under heaven,
　　　Which can make the dead arise,
　　　And exalt them to the skies.

That which Christ so hardly wrought,
That which He so dearly bought,
That salvation, mortals, say,
Will ye madly cast away?

Rather gladly for that Name
Bear the cross, endure the shame:
Joyfully for Him to die
Is not death, but victory.

Jesu, Who dost condescend
To be called the sinner's Friend,
Hear us as to Thee we pray,
Glorying in Thy Name to-day.

Glory to the Father be,
Glory, Holy Son, to Thee,
Glory to the Holy Ghost,
From the saints and angel-host.   Amen.

---

140 My God, how wonderful Thou art,
   Thy majesty how bright,
How beautiful Thy mercy-seat,
   In depths of burning light.

How dread are Thine eternal years,
   O everlasting Lord,
By prostrate spirits day and night
   Incessantly adored.

How wonderful, how beautiful,
  The sight of Thee must be,
Thine endless wisdom, boundless power,
  And awful purity.

O may I fear Thee, Living God,
  With deepest, tenderest fears,
And worship Thee with trembling hope,
  And penitential tears.

Yet I may love Thee too, O Lord,
  Almighty as Thou art,
For Thou has stooped to ask of me
  The love of my poor heart.

No earthly father loves like Thee,
  No mother, e'er so mild,
Bears and forbears as Thou hast done
  With me Thy sinful child.

Father of Jesus, love's reward,
  What rapture will it be,
Prostrate before Thy throne to lie,
  And ever gaze on Thee!   Amen.

---

141   Jesu, meek and lowly,
      Saviour, pure and holy,
      On Thy love relying,
      Hear me humbly crying.

Prince of life and power,
My salvation's Tower,
On the Cross I view Thee
Calling sinners to Thee.

There behold me gazing
At the sight amazing;
Bending low before Thee,
Helpless I adore Thee.

By Thy red wounds streaming,
With Thy life-blood gleaming,
Blood for sinners flowing,
Pardon free bestowing;

By that fount of blessing
Thy dear love expressing,
All my aching sadness
Turn Thou into gladness.

Lord in mercy guide me,
Be Thou e'er beside me;
In Thy ways direct me,
'Neath Thy wings protect me.
      Amen.

---

142 Jesu, meek and gentle,
Son of God most high,
Pitying, loving Saviour,
Hear Thy children's cry.

Pardon our offences,
Loose our captive chains,
Break down every idol
Which our soul detains.

Give us holy freedom,
Fill our hearts with love;
Draw us, Holy Jesus!
To the realms above.

Lead us on our journey,
Be Thyself the Way
Through terrestrial darkness
To celestial day.

Jesu, meek and gentle,
Son of God most high,
Pitying, loving Saviour,
Hear Thy children's cry. Amen.

---

143 Through all the changing scenes of life,
In trouble and in joy,
The praises of my God shall still
My heart and tongue employ.

O magnify the Lord with me
With me exalt His name;
When in distress to Him I called,
He to my rescue came.

The hosts of God encamp around
    The dwellings of the just;
Deliverance He affords to all
    Who on his succour trust.

O make but trial of His love,
    Experience will decide,
How bless'd are they, and only they,
    Who in His truth confide.

Fear Him, ye saints, and you will then
    Have nothing else to fear;
Make you His service your delight,
    Your wants shall be his care.

To Father, Son, and Holy Ghost,
    The God whom we adore,
Be glory, as it was, is now,
    And shall be evermore.   Amen.

---

144.   O worship the King,
       All glorious above;
    O gratefully sing
       His power and His love;
    Our Shield and Defender,
       The Ancient of days,
    Pavilioned in splendour,
       And girded with praise.

O tell of His might,
   O sing of His grace,
Whose robe is the light,
   Whose canopy space;
His chariots of wrath
   The thunder clouds form,
And dark is His path
   On the wings of the storm.

Frail children of dust,
   And feeble as frail,
In Thee do we trust,
   Nor find Thee to fail.
Thy mercies how tender!
   How firm to the end!
Our Maker, Defender,
   Redeemer and Friend.

O measureless Might,
   Ineffable love!
While angels delight
   To hymn Thee above,
Thy ransomed creation,
   Though feeble their lays,
With true adoration
   Shall sing to Thy praise.

145 All ye who seek for sure relief
   In trouble and distress,
Whatever sorrow vex the mind,
   Or guilt the soul oppress:

Jesus, who gave himself for you
   Upon the Cross to die,
Opens to you His sacred Heart:
   Oh, to that Heart draw nigh.

Ye hear how kindly He invites;
   Ye hear His words so blest;
"All ye that labour come to Me,
   And I will give you rest."

O Jesu, Joy of saints on high,
   Thou Hope of sinners here;
Attracted by those loving words
   To Thee I lift my prayer.

Wash Thou my wounds in that dear
      Blood
   Which forth from Thee doth flow;
New grace, new hope inspire; a new
   And better heart bestow.   Amen.

———

146 Songs of praise the angels sang,
   Heaven with Alleluias rang,
   When creation was begun,
   When God spake and it was done.

Songs of praise awoke the morn
When the Prince of Peace was born;
Songs of praise arose, when He
Captive led Captivity.

Heaven and earth must pass away,
Songs of praise shall crown that day:
God will make new heaven and earth,
Songs of praise shall hail their birth.

And will man alone be dumb
Till that glorious kingdom come?
No, the Church delights to raise
Psalms and hymns and songs of praise.

Saints below, with heart and voice,
Still in songs of praise rejoice;
Learning here, by faith and love,
Songs of praise to sing above.

Hymns of glory, songs of praise,
Father, unto Thee we raise;
Jesu, glory unto Thee,
With the Spirit, ever be.   Amen.

---

147 O God of Hosts, the mighty Lord,
    How lovely is the place,
Where Thou, enthroned in glory, shew'st
    The brightness of Thy face.

My longing soul faints with desire
   To view Thy blest abode;
My panting heart and flesh cry out
   For Thee the living God.

For in Thy Courts one single day
   'Tis better to attend,
Than, Lord, in any place besides
   A thousand days to spend.

O Lord of Hosts, my King and God,
   How highly blest are they,
Who in Thy temple always dwell,
   And There Thy praise display!

To Father, Son, and Holy Ghost,
   The God Whom we adore,
Be glory, as it was, is now,
   And shall be evermore. Amen.

When our heads are bowed with woe,
When the bitter tears o'erflow,
When we mourn the lost, the dear,
Jesu, Son of Mary, hear!

Thou, O Lord! our flesh hast worn,
Thou our mortal griefs hast borne,
Thou hast shed the human tear;
Jesu, Son of Mary, hear!

When the heart is sad within
With the thought of all its sin,
When the spirit shrinks with fear,
Jesu, Son of Mary, hear!

Thou the shame, the grief hast known,
Though the sins were not Thine Own,
Thou hast deigned their load to bear;
Jesu, Son of Mary, hear!

When the solemn death-bell tolls
For our own departing souls,
When our final doom is near,
Jesu, Son of Mary, hear!

Thou hast bowed the dying Head,
Thou the blood of life hast shed,
Thou hast filled a mortal bier;
Jesu, Son of Mary, hear!   Amen.

---

149   We love the place, O God,
Wherein Thine honour dwells;
The joy of Thine abode
All earthly joy excels.

It is the house of prayer,
Wherein Thy servants meet;
And Thou, O Lord, art there
Thy chosen flock to greet.

179.

We love the sacred Font;
For there the Holy Dove
To pour is ever wont
His blessing from above.

We love Thine Altar, Lord;
Oh what on earth so dear?
For there, in faith adored,
We find Thy Presence near.

We love the Word of Life.
The Word that tells of peace,
Of comfort in the strife,
And joys that never cease.

We love to sing below
For mercies freely given;
But oh! we long to know
The triumph-song of heaven.

Lord Jesus, give us grace
On earth to love Thee more,
In heaven to see Thy Face,
And with Thy saints adore.   Amen.

150 Take up thy cross, the Saviour said,
If thou wouldst My disciple be ;
Deny thyself, the world forsake,
And humbly follow after Me.

Take up thy cross; let not its weight
Fill thy weak spirit with alarm ;
His strength shall bear thy spirit up,
And brace thy heart, and nerve thine arm.

Take up thy cross, nor heed the shame;
Nor let thy foolish pride rebel:
Thy Lord for thee the Cross endured,
To save thy soul from death and hell.

Take up thy cross then in His strength,
And calmly every danger brave;
'Twill guide the to a better home,
And lead to victory o'er the grave.

Take up thy cross, and follow Christ,
Nor think till death to lay it down;
For only he, who bears the cross,
May hope to wear the glorious crown.

To Thee, great Lord, the One in Three
All praise for evermore ascend;
O grant us in our home to see
The heavenly life that knows no end.
                    Amen.

151   Behold the Lamb of God !
O Thou for sinners slain,
Let it not be in vain
      That Thou hast died :
Thee for my Saviour let me take,
My only refuge let me make
      Thy pierced Side.

     Behold the Lamb of God !
Into the sacred flood
Of Thy most precious Blood
      My soul I cast :
Wash me and make me clean within,
And keep me pure from every sin,
      Till life be past.

     Behold the Lamb of God !
All hail, Incarnate WORD,
Thou everlasting Lord,
      Saviour most blest;
Fill us with love that never faints,
Grant us with all Thy blessed Saints
      Eternal rest.

     Behold the Lamb of God !
Worthy is He alone,
That sitteth on the throne
      Of God above :
One with the Ancient of all days,
One with the Comforter in praise,
      All Light and Love.   Amen.

152 The roseate hues of early dawn,
   The brightness of the day,
The crimson of the sunset sky,
   How fast they fade away!
Oh, for the pearly gates of heaven,
   Oh, for the golden floor,
Oh, for the Sun of Righteousness
   That setteth nevermore!

The highest hopes we cherish here,
   How fast they tire and faint;
How many a spot defiles the robe
   That wraps an earthly saint!
Oh, for a heart that never sins,
   Oh, for a soul washed white,
Oh, for a voice to praise our King,
   Nor weary day nor night.

Here faith is ours, and heavenly hope,
   And grace to lead us higher;
But there are perfectness, and peace,
   Beyond our best desire.
Oh, by Thy love, and anguish, Lord,
   And by Thy life laid down,
Grant that we fall not from Thy grace,
   Nor cast away our crown.   Amen.

153 Blest are the pure in heart
   For they shall see our God ;
The secret of the Lord is theirs;
   Their soul is Christ's abode.

   The Lord, Who left the heavens
   Our life and peace to bring,
To dwell in lowliness with men,
   Their Pattern and their King;

   He to the lowly soul
   Doth still Himself impart,
And for His dwelling and his Throne
   Chooseth the pure in heart.

   Lord, we Thy presence seek;
   May ours this blessing be;
Give us a pure and lowly heart,
   A temple meet for Thee.

   All glory, Lord, to Thee,
   Whom heaven and earth adore,
To Father, Son, and Holy Ghost,
   One God for evermore.   Amen.

---

154 To the Name of our Salvation
      Laud and honour let us pay;
   Which for many a generation
      Hid in God's foreknowledge lay,
   But with holy exultation
      We may sing aloud to-day.

Jesus is the name we treasure;
  Name beyond what words can tell;
Name of gladness, Name of pleasure,
  Ear and heart delighting well;
Name of sweetness, passing measure,
  Saving us from sin and hell.

'Tis the Name for adoration,
  Name for songs of victory,
Name for holy meditation
  In this vale of misery,
Name for joyful veneration
  By the citizens on high.

'Tis the Name that whoso preacheth
  Speaks like music to the ear;
Who in prayer this Name beseecheth
  Sweetest comfort findeth near;
Who its perfect wisdom reacheth
  Heavenly joy possesseth here.

Jesus is the Name exalted
  Over every other name;
In this Name, whene'er assaulted,
  We can put our foes to shame;
Strength to them who else had halted,
  Eyes to blind, and feet to lame.

Therefore we in love adoring
  This most blessed Name revere;
Holy Jesu, Thee imploring
  So to write it in us here;
That hereafter heavenward soaring
  We may sing with angels there.
                          Amen.

155 Let Saints below join Saints above,
   To whom their Rest is given;
And on the eagle wings of love
   Soar towards the joys of Heaven.

Let Saints on earth in concert sing,
   With those whose work is done;
For all the servants of our King
   In every place are One.

One Family, we dwell in Him,
   One Church, above, beneath;
Though now divided by the stream,
   The narrow stream of death.

One Army of the Living God,
   To His command we bow :
Part of the Host have crossed the flood,
   And part are crossing now.

E'en now to their eternal Home
   There pass some spirits blest;
While others to the margin come,
   Waiting their call to Rest.

Jesu, be Thou our constant Guide;
   Then, when the word is given,
Bid Jordan's narrow stream divide,
   And give us Rest in Heaven.   Amen.

156 My God, my Father, while I stray
　　Far from my home in life's rough way,
　　O teach me from my heart to say,
　　　　　　"Thy will be done."

　　Though dark my path, and sad my lot,
　　Let me be still and murmur not,
　　Or breathe the prayer divinely taught,
　　　　　　"Thy will be done."

　　What though in lonely grief I sigh
　　For friends beloved no longer nigh,
　　Submissive would I still reply,
　　　　　　"Thy will be done."

　　If Thou shouldst call me to resign
　　What most I prize, it ne'er was mine;
　　I only yield Thee what is Thine;
　　　　　　"Thy will be done."

　　Let but my fainting heart be blest
　　With Thy sweet Spirit for its guest,
　　My God, to Thee I leave the rest;
　　　　　　"Thy will be done."

　　Renew my will from day to day,
　　Blend it with Thine, and take away
　　All that now makes it hard to say,
　　　　　　"Thy will be done."
　　　　　　　　　　　Amen.

157 O Love, Who formedst me to wear
    The image of Thy Godhead here;
Who soughtest me with tender care
    Through all my wanderings wild and drear;
O Love, I give myself to Thee,
Thine ever, only Thine to be.

O Love, Who e'er life's earliest dawn
    On me Thy choice hast gently laid;
O Love, Who here as Man wast born,
    And wholly like to us wast made;
O Love, I give myself to Thee,
Thine ever, only Thine to be.

O Love, Who once in time wast slain, [woe;
    Pierced through and through with bitter
O Love, Who wrestling thus didst gain
    That we eternal joy might know;
O love, I give myself to Thee,
Thine ever, only Thine to be.

O Love, Who lovest me for aye,
    Who for my soul dost ever plead;
O Love, Who didst my ransom pay,
    Whose power sufficeth in my stead;
O Love, I give myself to Thee,
Thine ever, only Thine to be.

O Love, Who once shalt bid me rise
    From out this dying life of ours;
O Love, Who once o'er yonder skies
    Shalt set me in the fadeless bowers;
O love, I give myself to thee,
Thine ever, only Thine to be.   Amen.

158 Hosanna to the living Lord!
Hosanna to the Incarnate Word!
To Christ, Creator, Saviour, King,
Let earth, let heaven hosanna sing.
    Hosanna in the highest!

O Saviour, with protecting care
Abide in this Thy house of prayer,
Where we Thy parting promise claim
Assembled in Thy sacred Name.
    Hosanna in the highest!

But chiefest, in our cleansed breast
Bid Thine eternal Spirit rest;
And make our secret soul to be
A temple pure, and worthy Thee.
    Hosanna in the highest!

To God the Father, God the Son,
And God the Spirit, Three in One,
Be honour, praise, and glory given
By all on earth, and all in Heaven.
    Hosanna in the highest!   Amen.

---

159 Praise the Lord! ye heavens, adore Him,
  Praise Him, angels, in the height:
Sun and moon, rejoice before Him,
  Praise Him, all ye stars and light:

Praise the Lord ! for He hath spoken,
  Worlds His mighty voice obeyed;
Laws, which never shall be broken,
  For their guidance He hath made.

Praise the Lord ! for He is glorious;
  Never shall His promise fail;
God hath made His saints victorious,
  Sin and death shall not prevail.
Praise the God of our salvation;
  Hosts on high, His power proclaim;
Heaven and earth, and all creation,
  Laud and magnify His Name !   Amen.

---

160   Oft in danger, oft in woe,
        Onward Christians, onward go;
        Bear the toil, maintain the strife,
        Strengthened with the Bread of Life.

        Let not sorrow dim your eye,
        Soon shall every tear be dry;
        Let not fear your course impede,
        Great your strength, if great your need.

        Let your drooping hearts be glad;
        March in heavenly armour glad;
        Fight, nor think the battle long,
        Soon shall victory wake your song.

Onward then to glory move;
More than conquerors ye shall prove;
Though opposed by many a foe,
Christian soldiers, onward go!

Hymns of glory and of praise,
Father, unto Thee we raise;
Holy Jesus, praise to Thee
With the Spirit ever be.   Amen.

---

161 Jesu, grant me this, I pray,
Ever in Thy Heart to stay;
Let me evermore abide
Hidden in Thy wounded Side.

If the evil one prepare,
Or the world, a tempting snare,
I am safe when I abide
In Thy Heart and wounded Side.

If the flesh, more dangerous still,
Tempt my soul to deeds of ill,
Naught I fear when I abide
In Thy Heart and wounded Side.

Death will come one day to me;
Jesu, cast me not from Thee:
Dying let me still abide
In Thy Heart and wounded Side.
                              Amen.

162 Jesu, Lover of my soul,
   Let me to Thy Bosom fly,
While the gathering waters roll,
   While the tempest still is high:
Hide me, O my Saviour, hide;
   Till the storm of life be past;
Safe into the haven guide,
   O receive my soul at last.

Other refuge have I none;
   Hangs my helpless soul on Thee:
Leave, ah! leave me not alone,
   Still support and comfort me.
All my trust on Thee is stayed,
   All my help from Thee I bring;
Cover my defenceless head
   With the shadow of Thy wing.

Plenteous grace with Thee is found,
   Grace to cleanse from every sin;
Let the healing streams abound,
   Make and keep me pure within:
Thou of Life the Fountain art,
   Freely let me take of Thee;
Spring Thou up within my heart,
   Rise to all eternity.   Amen.

———

163 Jerusalem, my happy home,
      Name ever dear to me,
   When shall my labours have an end?
      Thy joys when shall I see?

When shall these eyes Thy heaven-built
   walls
  And pearly gates behold ?
Thy bulwarks, with salvation strong,
  And streets of shining gold ?

Apostles, Martyrs, Prophets, there
  Around my Saviour stand;
And all I love in Christ below
  Will join the glorious band.

Jerusalem, my happy home,
  When shall I come to thee ?
When shall my labours have an end ?
  Thy joys when shall I see ?

O Christ, do Thou my soul prepare
  For that bright home of love;
That I may see Thee and adore,
  With all Thy saints above.   Amen.

---

164   Soldiers of Christ, arise,
      And put your armour on,
Strong in the strength which God supplies
  Through His Eternal Son:

  Strong in the Lord of Hosts,
    And in His mighty power;
Who in the strength of Jesus trusts
  Is more than conqueror.

Stand then in His great might,
  With all His strength endued;
And take, to arm you for the fight,
  The panoply of God.

From strength to strength go on,
  Wrestle, and fight, and pray;
Tread all the powers of darkness down,
  And win the well-fought day.

That having all things done,
  And all your conflicts past,
Ye may obtain, through Christ alone,
  A crown of joy at last.

Jesu, Eternal Son,
  We praise Thee and adore,
Who art with God the Father One
  And Spirit evermore. Amen.

---

165   There is a blessed Home
  Beyond this land of woe,
  Where trials never come,
  Nor tears of sorrow flow;
  Where faith is lost in sight,
  And patient hope is crowned,
  And everlasting light
  Its glory throws around.

There is a land of peace,
Good angels know it well;
Glad songs that never cease
Within its portals swell;
Around its glorious Throne
Ten thousand saints adore
Christ, with the Father One
And Spirit, evermore.

O joy all joys beyond,
To see the Lamb Who died,
And count each sacred Wound
In Hands, and Feet, and Side;
To give to Him the praise
Of every triumph won,
And sing through endless days
The great things He hath done.

Look up ye saints of God,
Nor fear to tread below
The path your Saviour trod
Of daily toil and woe;
Wait but a little while
In uncomplaining love,
His own most gracious smile
Shall welcome you above.   Amen.

---

166 Lord, as to Thy dear Cross we flee,
    And plead to be forgiven,
So let Thy life our pattern be
    And form our souls for heaven.

Help us, through good report and ill,
   Our daily cross to bear;
Like Thee, to do our Father's will,
   Our brethren's griefs to share.

Let grace our selfishness expel,
   Our earthliness refine :
And kindness in our bosoms dwell,
   As free and true as Thine.

If joy shall at Thy bidding fly,
   And grief's dark day come on,
We in our turn would meekly cry,
   "Father, Thy will be done."

Kept peaceful in the midst of strife,
   Forgiving and forgiven,
O may we lead the pilgrim's life,
   And follow Thee to Heaven.   Amen.

---

167 Ye servants of the Lord,
   Each in his office, wait,
Observant of His heavenly word,
   And watchful at His gate.

Let all your lamps be bright,
   And trim the golden flame;
Gird up your loins as in His sight,
   For awful is His Name.

Watch! 'tis your Lord's command,
   And while we speak He's near;
Mark the first signal of His hand,
   And ready all appear.

O happy servant he,
   In such a posture found;
He shall his Lord with rapture see,
   And be with honour crowned.

Christ shall the banquet spread
   With His own royal Hand,
And raise that faithful servant's head
   Amid His angel-band.

All glory, Lord, to Thee.
   Whom heaven and earth adore;
To Father, Son, and Holy Ghost,
   One God for evermore.   Amen.

---

168 How sweet the Name of Jesus sounds
   In a believer's ear!
It soothes his sorrows, heals his wounds,
   And drives away his fear.

It makes the wounded spirit whole,
   And calms the troubled breast;
'Tis manna to the hungry soul,
   And to the weary rest.

Dear Name ! the rock on which I build,
  My shield and hiding-place,
My never-failing treasury, filled
  With boundless stores of grace.

Jesu ! my Shepherd, Husband, Friend,
  My Prophet, Priest, and King,
My Lord, my Life, my Way, mine End,
  Accept the praise I bring.

Weak is the effort of my heart,
  And cold my warmest thought;
But when I see Thee as Thou art
  I'll praise Thee as I ought.

Till then I would Thy love proclaim
  With every fleeting breath;
And may the music of Thy Name
  Refresh my soul in death.   Amen.

---

169 O help us, Lord, each hour of need
      Thy heavenly succour give;
    Help us in thought, and word, and deed,
      Each hour on earth we live.

    O help us when our spirits bleed
      With contrite anguish sore;
    And when our hearts are cold and dead,
      O help us, Lord, the more.

O help us through the prayer of faith,
    More firmly to believe;
For still the more the servant hath,
    The more shall he receive.

O help us, Jesu, from on high;
    We know no help but Thee;
O help us so to live and die
    As Thine in heaven to be. Amen.

---

170 O Lord, how joyful 'tis to see
    The brethren join in love to Thee;
    On Thee alone their heart relies,
    Their only strength Thy grace supplies.

    How sweet, within Thy holy place,
    With one accord to sing Thy grace,
    Besieging Thine attentive ear
    With all the force of fervent prayer.

    O may we love the house of God,
    Of peace and joy the blest abode;
    O may no angry strife destroy
    That sacred peace, that holy joy.

    The world without may rage, but we
    Will only cling more close to Thee,
    With hearts to Thee more wholly given,
    More weaned from earth, more fixed on heaven.

Lord, shower upon us from above
The sacred gift of mutual love ;
Each other's wants may we supply,
And reign together in the sky. Amen.

---

171 God moves in a mysterious way,
    His wonders to perform ;
He plants His footsteps in the sea,
    And rides upon the storm.

Deep in unfathomable mines
    Of never-failing skill
He treasures up His bright designs,
    And works His sovereign will.

Ye fearful saints, fresh courage take;
    The clouds ye so much dread
Are big with mercy, and shall break
    In blessings on your head.

Judge not the Lord by feeble sense,
    But trust Him for His grace :
Behind a frowning providence
    He hides a smiling face.

Blind unbelief is sure to err,
    And scan His work in vain;
God is His own interpreter,
    And He will make it plain. Amen.

172 Let every heart exulting beat
With joy at Jesu's Name of bliss;
With every pure delight replete,
And passing sweet, its music is.

Jesus the comfortless consoles,
Jesus each sinful fever quells;
Jesus the power of hell controls,
Jesus each deadly foe repels.

O speak His glorious Name abroad!
Jesus let every tongue confess;
Let every heart and voice accord
The Healer of our souls to bless.

Jesu, the sinner's Friend, abide
With us, and hearken to our prayer;
Thy frail and erring wanderers guide,
In mercy our transgressions spare.

All might, all glory be to Thee
Refulgent with this name Divine;
All honour, worship, majesty,
Jesu, for evermore be Thine.   Amen.

---

173   To Christ the Prince of peace
And Son of God most high,
The Father of the world to come,
We lift our joyful cry.

Deep in His Heart for us
  The wound of love He bore,
That love which still He kindles in
  The hearts that Him adore.

O Jesu, Victim blest,
  What else but love divine
Could Thee constrain to open thus,
  That Sacred Heart of Thine?

O Fount of endless life,
  O Spring of water clear!
O flame celestial, cleansing all
  Who unto Thee draw near!

Hide me in Thy dear Heart,
  For thither do I fly;
There seek Thy grace through life, in death
Thine immortality.   Amen.

---

174 Jesus shall reign where'er the sun
Doth his successive journeys run :
His kingdom stretch from shore to shore,
Till moons shall wax and wane no more.

People and realms of every tongue
Dwell on his love with sweetest song,
And infant voices shall proclaim
Their early blessings on His Name.

Blessings abound where'er He reigns;
The prisoner leaps to loose his chains;
The weary find eternal rest,
And all the sons of want are blest.

Let every creature rise and bring
Peculiar honours to our King;
Angels descend with songs again,
And earth repeat the loud Amen.   Amen.

---

175 O God, our help in ages past,
    Our hope for years to come,
  Our shelter from the stormy blast,
    And our eternal home!

  Beneath the shadow of Thy Throne
    Thy saints have dwelt secure;
  Sufficient is Thine arm alone,
    And our defence is sure.

  Before the hills in order stood,
    Or earth received her frame,
  From everlasting Thou art God,
    To endless years the same.

  A thousand ages in Thy sight
    Are like an evening gone;
  Short as the watch that ends the night
    Before the rising sun.

Time, like an ever-rolling stream,
   Bears all its sons away;
They fly forgotten, as a dream
   Dies at the opening day.

O God, our help in ages past,
   Our hope for years to come;
Be Thou our guard while troubles last,
   And our eternal home.   Amen.

---

176 Praise my soul, the King of Heaven,
   To His feet thy tribute bring;
Ransomed, healed, restored, forgiven,
   Evermore His praises sing,
     Alleluia ! Alleluia !
Praise the everlasting King.

Praise Him for His grace and favour
   To our fathers in distress;
Praise Him still the same as ever,
   Slow to chide, and swift to bless :
     Alleluia ! Alleluia !
Glorious in His faithfulness.

Father-like, he tends and spares us,
   Well our feeble frame He knows;
In His hands He gently bears us,
   Rescues us from all our foes;
     Alleluia ! Alleluia !
Widely yet His mercy flows.

Angels in the height adore Him!
Ye behold Him face to face;
Saints triumphant bow before Him!
Gathered in from every race:
Alleluia! Alleluia!
Praise with us the God of grace.
       Amen.

---

177 Nearer, my God, to Thee,
   Nearer to Thee;
E'en though it be a cross
  That raiseth me,
Still all my song shall be,
Nearer, my God, to Thee,
  Nearer to Thee!

Though, like a wanderer,
   The sun gone down,
Darkness comes over me,
  My rest a stone:
Yet in my dreams I'd be
Nearer, my God, to Thee,
  Nearer to Thee!

There let my way appear
   Steps unto heaven;
All that Thou sendest me
  In mercy given:
Angels to beckon me
Nearer, my God, to Thee,
  Nearer to Thee!

Then, with my waking thoughts
    Bright with Thy praise,
Out of my stony griefs
    Bethel I'll raise;
So by my woes to be
Nearer, my God, to Thee,
    Nearer to Thee! Amen.

THE TRANSFIGURATION, 6TH AUG.

178 O wondrous type, O vision fair
Of glory that the Church shall share,
Which Christ upon the mountain shows,
Where brighter than the sun He glows!

From age to age the tale declare,
How with the three disciples there,
Where Moses and Elias meet,
The Lord holds converse high and sweet.

The law and prophets there have place,
Two chosen witnesses of grace;
The Father's voice from out the cloud
Proclaims His Only Son aloud.

With shining Face and bright array,
Christ deigns to manifest to-day
What glory shall be theirs above,
Who joy in God with perfect love.

And faithful hearts are raised on high
By this great vision's mystery,
For which in joyful strains we raise
The voice of prayer, the hymn of praise.

O Father, with the Eternal Son
And Holy Spirit, ever One,
Vouchsafe to bring us by Thy grace
To see Thy glory face to face.   Amen.

---

179   Alike in happiness or woe,
    Lord! we will follow Thee;
And tread the path Thyself didst go,
    Whate'er that path may be.

With earnest zeal 'twas Thy delight
    To do Thy Father's will :
O may such zeal our souls excite,
    His precepts to fulfil.

If in some dark affliction's day
    Our path through sorrow run,
May we, like Thee, have grace to say,
    "Thy will, O Lord, be done."

In Thee a sacred burning Love
    In all Thy course did shine;
O may such love in us too prove
    That we, O Lord, are Thine.

Supported by Almighty Grace,
  We'll tread Thy heavenly road,
And carefully Thy footsteps trace,
  Which lead to Thine abode.

Now let the Father, and the Son,
  And Spirit, be adored,
Where there are works to make Him
      known,
  Or Saints to love the Lord.   Amen.

180 The Saviour comes; no outward pomp
  Bespeaks His Presence high,
No earthly beauty shines in Him
  To draw the carnal eye.

Rejected and despised of men,
  Behold a Man of woe!
Grief was His heavy burden here
  Through all His life below.

Yet all the griefs He felt were ours,
  And ours the woes He bore;
Pangs, not His Own, His spotless Soul
  With bitter anguish tore.

His sacred Blood hath washed our souls
  From sin's polluting stain;
His Stripes have healed us, and His Death
  Revived our souls again.

We all like sheep have gone astray
　In ruin's fatal road :
On Him were man's transgressions laid;
　He bore the mighty load.

He died to bear the guilt of men,
　That sin might be forgiven;
He lives to bless them, and defend,
　And plead their cause in Heaven.

To God the Son, Who lowly came
　Lost sinners to restore,
All glory to His holy Name,
　All glory evermore. Amen.

181　There is a Book who runs may read,
　　Which heavenly truth imparts;
　And all the lore its scholars need,
　　Pure eyes and Christian hearts.

　The works of God above below,
　　Within us, and around,
　Are pages in that book to show
　　How God Himself is found.

　The glorious sky embracing all
　　Is like the Maker's Love,
　Wherewith encompassed great and small
　　In peace and order move.

The moon above, the Church below,
  A wondrous race they run;
And all their radiance, all their glow,
  Each borrows of its Sun.

The Saviour lends the light and heat,
  That crowns His holy hill;
The Saints, like stars, around His Seat
  Perform their courses still.

Thou Who hast given me eyes to see,
  And love this sight so fair,
Give me a heart to find out Thee,
  And read Thee everywhere.

To God the Father, God the Son,
  And God the Holy Ghost,
All honour by the Church be done,
  And by the heavenly host.   Amen.

182 My God, I love Thee, not because
  I hope for Heaven thereby;
Nor yet because who love Thee not
  Must burn eternally.

Thou, O my Jesu! Thou didst me
  Upon the Cross embrace;
For me didst bear the nails and spear,
  And manifold disgrace:

And griefs and torments numberless,
　And sweat of agony;
E'en death itself—and all for me
　Who was Thine enemy.

Then why, O Blessed Jesu Christ!
　Should I not love Thee well?
Not for the sake of winning Heaven,
　Or of escaping Hell.

Not with the hope of gaining aught;
　Not seeking a reward;
But as Thyself hast loved me,
　O ever loving Lord.

E'en so I love Thee, and will love,
　And in Thy praise will sing;
Solely because Thou art my God,
　And my eternal King.　Amen.

183　Ye boundless realms of joy,
　　Exalt your Maker's fame;
　His praise your song employ
　　Above the starry frame;
　　　Your voices raise,
　　　Ye Cherubim,
　　　And Seraphim,
　　　To sing His praise.

United zeal be shown,
  His wondrous fame to raise,
Whose glorious Name alone,
  Deserves our endless praise:
    Earth's utmost ends
    His power obey;
    His glorious sway
    The sky transcends.

His chosen Saints to grace,
  He sets them up on high,
And favours Israel's race
  Who still to Him are nigh:
    O therefore raise
    Your grateful voice,
    And still rejoice
    The Lord to praise.

To God the Father, Son,
  And Spirit ever blest,
Eternal Three in One,
  All worship be addrest;
    As heretofore
    It was, is now,
    And shall be so
    For evermore.   Amen.

184 I worship Thee, sweet Will of God,
 And all Thy ways adore,
And every day I live, I seem
 To love Thee more and more.

I love to kiss each print where Thou
 Hast set Thine unseen feet;
I cannot fear Thee, blessed Will,
 Thine empire is so sweet.

I have no cares, O blessed Will,
 For all my cares are Thine;
I live in triumph, Lord, for Thou
 Hast made Thy triumphs mine.

He always wins who sides with God,
 To him no chance is lost;
God's Will is sweetest to him when
 It triumphs at his cost.

Ill that He blesses is our good,
 And unblest good is ill;
And all is right that seems most wrong,
 If it be His sweet Will. Amen.

---

185 Holiest, breathe an ev'ning blessing,
 Ere repose our spirits seal;
Sin and want we come confessing:
 Thou canst save, and Thou canst heal.

Though the night be dark and dreary,
Darkness cannot hide from Thee;
Thou art He Who, never weary,
Watchest where Thy people be.

Though destruction walk around us,
Though the arrow past us fly,
Angel guards from Thee surround us;
We are safe if They art nigh.

Should swift death this night o'ertake us,
And our couch become our tomb,
May the morn in Heaven awake us,
Clad in light and deathless bloom. Amen.

186 Wouldst thou enjoy the eternal years
With Christ, beyond the shining spheres?
Count well the cost, nor think to gain
That bliss without a passing pain.

For thee Thy Lord bore heaven's loss,
For thee endured the shameful Cross,
Scorn, pain, and agonizing throe,
To save thee from eternal woe.

And 'tis thy Lord's mysterious will,
That all, His heavenly courts who fill,
Should suffer now, for Jesu's sake,
Ere they His endless bliss partake.

Look well then on thy suffering Lord,
Study His every act and word;
Take up thy Cross with reverend care
In meekness after Him to bear.

Keen though the sorrow, sharp the grief,
Jesu can give thee sweet relief,
All earthly things are but as dross,
Viewed in the mirror of the Cross.

Yea, Jesu! every pang shall be
But light, which we can bear for Thee;
Our keenest woe to joy shall turn
If Thy blest love within us burn.

To God the Father, God the Son,
And God the Spirit, Three in One;
Be praise and adoration given,
By all on earth and all in heaven. Amen.

---

187 Sweet Saviour, bless us ere we go;
    Thy word into our minds instil;
And make our lukewarm hearts to glow
    With lowly love and fervent will,
Through life's long day and death's dark night,
    O gentle Jesu, be our Light.

The day is gone, its hours have run,
  And Thou hast taken count of all,
The scanty triumphs grace hath won,
  The broken vow, the frequent fall.
Through life's long day and death's dark
    night,
O gentle Jesu, be our Light.

Grant us, dear Lord, from evil ways
  True absolution and release;
And bless us, more than in past days,
  With purity and inward peace.
Through life's long day and death's dark
    night,
O gentle Jesu, be our Light.

Do more than pardon, give us joy,
  Sweet fear, and sober liberty,
And simple hearts without alloy
  That only long to be like Thee.
Through life's long day and death's dark
    night,
O gentle Jesu, be our Light.

Labour is sweet, for Thou hast toiled;
  And care is light, for Thou hast cared;
Ah! never let our works be soiled
  With strife, or by deceit ensnared.
Through life's long day and death's dark
    night,
O gentle Jesu, be our Light.

For all we love, the poor, the sad,
   The sinful, unto Thee we call ;
O let Thy mercy make us glad:
   Thou art our Jesus, and our All.
Through life's long day and death's dark
      night,
O gentle Jesu, be our Light.   Amen.

---

188   O Father! Who didst all things make,
   That heaven and earth might do Thy will,
Bless us this eve for Jesu's sake,
   And for Thy work preserve us still.

O Son! Who didst redeem mankind,
   And set the captive sinner free,
Keep us this eve with peaceful mind,
   That we may safe abide with Thee.

O Holy Ghost! Who by Thy power,
   The Church elect dost sanctify,
Seal us this eve, and hour by hour
   Our hearts and members purify.

Praise be to Father, praise to Son,
   Blest Spirit, equal praise to Thee;
Glory to God, the Three in One;
   Glory to God, the One in Three.   Amen.

189 O gracious Hand, that freely gives
   The fruits of earth, our toil to bless,
O Love, by which the sinner lives!
   O let our tongues that love confess.

Our God for all our need provides;
   His sun o'er all alike doth shine;
From none His glorious beams He hides;
   So will the Father's Love Divine.

Again His Love our garners fills,
   This Love again let all adore:
The cry of want His bounty stills,
   Who biddeth all His Name implore.

O may our lives through grace abound
   In fruits of Holiness and love;
Let all His courts with praise resound,
   To echo Angels' praise above.

Lord! when Thou shalt descend from Heaven,
   Thy ransomed harvest here to reap,
O in that day Thy joy be given
   To us, who now go forth to weep!

May none those hours of sadness loath,
   May none disdain in tears to sow:
Soon shall rejoicing crown the morn,
   To hearts that sorrow here below.

Praise God, from Whom all blessings flow,
  Praise Him above, Angelic Host;
Praise Him, all creatures here below,
  Praise Father, Son, and Holy Ghost.
                    Amen.

———

I know that my Redeemer lives;
  He lives, Who once was dead;
Peace to my troubled soul He gives,
  The "Peace" Himself hath said.

He lives, triumphant o'er the grave,
  All glorious in the sky;
He lives, eternally to save,
  Exalted now on high.

He lives, to bless me with His Love,
  My hungry soul to feed:
He lives, to plead for me above,
  To help in time of need.

I know that my Redeemer lives,
  He liveth still the same;
Peace to my troubled soul He gives;
  All glory to His Name.

Glory to Father and to Son,
  For in His Life we live;
Let equal praise to Him be done,
  Who on that life doth give.   Amen.

EASTER.

O Sons redeemed, this day we sing
The King of Heaven, the glorious King,
Whose rising makes creation ring.
                      Alleluia!

On the first morning of the week,
Before the day began to break,
They went their buried Lord to seek.
                      Alleluia!

The holy women, faithful three,
Soon as the Sabbath set them free,
T' embalm His Corpse came lovingly.
                      Alleluia!

An angel clad in white was he
That sat and spake unto the three—
"Your Lord is gone to Galilee."
                      Alleluia!

The dearly loved Apostle, John,
Ran foremost; Peter, following on,
First entered in—but Christ was gone!
                      Alleluia!

That night th' Apostles met in fear;—
Amidst them came their Lord most dear,
And said, "Peace be unto all here."
                      Alleluia!

When Didymus had after heard
That Jesus had fulfilled His word,
He doubted if it were the Lord.
                      Alleluia!

"Thomas, behold My Side," saith He,
"My .... My Flesh, My Body see,
And doubt not, but believe in Me."
                                    Alleluia!

He saw the Feet, the Hands, the Side,
No longer Thomas then denied,
"Thou art my Lord and God," he cried.
                                    Alleluia!

Blessed are they who have not seen,
And yet whose faith hath constant been,
In life eternal they shall reign.
                                    Alleluia!

In this most holy day of days,
Be laud, and jubilee, and praise,
To God both ....
                                    Alleluia!

Our humble thanks to God we pay,
For all His gifts this blessed day,
Gifts greater than all tongues can say.
                                    Alleluia. Amen.

192 And now the day is past and gone,
       O Lord! we lowly bow to Thee;
     Again as nightly shades come on,
       We to Thy sheltering Side do flee.

For all the ills this day hath done
  O let ~~us~~ ~~white~~ ~~appear~~ ~~Blooded~~
And keep us from the wicked one,
  Whom of ourselves we cannot heed.

Ravening he prowls Thy fold around,
  Aye watchful ~~on his~~ ~~sheep to spring~~
Father, this night let us be found
  Beneath the shadow of Thy wing.

Oh! when shall that Thy day have
    come,
  The day ne'er sinking to the west!
That country and that holy home, and
  Where foe no more shall be our
    rest!

Now to the Father and the Son
  Our feeble voice we humbly raise,
With Holy Spirit, Three in One,
  And hymn from age to age His praise.
                              Amen.

---

193 Jesu! Refuge of the weary,
    Object of the Spirit's love,
  Fountain in life's desert dreary,
    Saviour from the Ox-hot Above.

O how oft Thine eyes offended
  Gaze upon the sinner's fall;
Yet Thou on the Cross extended
  Bore the penalty of all.

Still we pass that Cross unheeding,
  Breathing no repentant vow,
Though we see Thee wounded, bleeding,
  And Thy thorn-encircled brow.

Yet Thy sinless Death hath bought us
  Life eternal, peace, and rest;
What Thy grace alone hath taught us
  Calms the sinner's stormy breast.

Jesu! would our hearts were burning
  With more fervent love for Thee;
Would our eyes were ever turning
  To Thy Cross of agony.

So in pain and rapture blending,
  Failing eyesight might grow dim,
While the heart would soar ascending
  To the circling Cherubim.

Then in glory, parted never
  From the blessed Saviour's side,
Graven on our hearts for ever
  Be the Cross and Crucified. Amen.

194 Sweet the moments, rich in blessing,
   Which before the Cross I spend;
Life and health and peace possessing,
   Through the sinner's dying Friend.
Kneel we now in wonder viewing
   Mercy's streams in streams of Blood;
Precious drops, our souls bedewing,
   From the all-cleansing, healing flood.

Love and grief our hearts dividing,
   Gazing here we'd spend our breath;
Constant still in faith abiding,
   Life deriving from His death.
Lord, in ceaseless contemplation
   Fix our hearts and eyes on Thine,
Till we taste Thy whole salvation,
   Where unveiled Thy glories shine.

For Thy sorrows we adore Thee,
   For the griefs that wrought our peace;
Gracious Saviour, we implore Thee,
   In our hearts Thy love increase.
Unto Thee, the world's Salvation,
   Father, Spirit, unto Thee
Low we bow in adoration,
   Ever blessed One and Three.   Amen.

195 Christian soul, dost thou desire
    Days of joy, and peace, and truth?
Learn to bear the yoke of Jesus,
    In the spring-tide of thy youth.

It may seem at first a burden,
    But the Lord will make it light;
He Himself will bear it with thee;
    He will ease it of its weight.

Only bear it well, and daily
    Thou wilt learn that yoke to love;
Strength and grace it here will bring thee
    And a bright reward above.

Glory be to God the Father,
    Glory to the Only Son,
Glory to the Holy Spirit,
    While eternal ages run.   Amen.

---

196 Holy Jesu! Saviour bless'd!
As, by passion strong possess'd,
Through this world of sin we stray,
Thou to guide us art the Way.

Holy Jesu! when the night
Of error blinds our clouded sight,
Round the cheering day to throw,
Saviour! then the Truth art Thou.

Holy Jesu! when our power
Fails us in temptation's hour,
All unequal to the strife,
Thou to aid us art the Life.

Who would reach his heavenly home,
Who would to the Father come,
Who the Father's presence see,
Jesu! he must come by Thee.

Channel of the Father's Grace!
Image of the Father's Face!
Saviour bless'd! Incarnate Son!
With the Father, Thou art One.

Glory to the Father be;
Glory, only Son, to Thee;
And, of equal power confess'd,
Glory to the Spirit bless'd.   Amen.

---

197 Lord of our life, and God of our salvation,
Star of our night, and hope of every nation,
Hear and receive Thy Church's supplication,
    Lord God Almighty.

See round Thine ark the angry billows curling,
See how Thy foes their banners are unfurling;
Lord, while their darts envenomed they are hurling,
    Thou canst preserve us.

Lord, Thou canst help when earthly armour faileth,
Lord, Thou canst save when deadly sin assaileth,
Lord, o'er Thy Rock nor death nor hell prevaileth;
    Grant us Thy peace, Lord!

Peace in our hearts, our evil thoughts assuaging,
Peace in Thy Church, where brothers are engaging,
Peace, when the world its busy war is waging;
    Calm Thy foes raging:

Grant us Thy help till backward they are driven,
Grant them Thy truth, that they may be forgiven,
Grant peace on earth, or, after we have striven,
    Peace in Thy heaven. Amen.

198 Hail, Thou once despised Jesus!
    Hail, Thou Galilean King!
Thou didst suffer to release us,
    Thou didst free salvation bring.

Paschal Lamb! by God appointed,
    All on Thee our sins were laid;
By Almighty Love anointed,
    Thou hast full atonement made.

All thy people are forgiven
    Through the virtue of Thy Blood;
Open'd is the gate of Heaven,
    Peace is made 'twixt man and God

Jesu, hail! enthroned in glory,
    There for ever to abide;
All the Angel hosts adore Thee,
    Seated at Thy Father's side.

There for sinners Thou art pleading,
    Spare them yet another year;
There for Saints art interceding,
    Till in glory they appear.

Worship, honour, power, and blessing,
    Thou art worthy to receive;
Loudest praises without ceasing,
    Meet it is for us to give.   Amen.

199 Days and moments quickly flying,
    Blend the living with the dead;
Soon will you and I be lying
    Each within our narrow bed.

Soon our souls to God who gave them
    Will have sped their rapid flight!
Able now by grace to save them,
    O! that, while we can, we might!

Jesu! infinite Redeemer!
    Maker of this mighty frame,
Teach, O teach us to remember
    What we are, and whence we came.

Whence we came and whither wending,
    Soon we must through darkness go,
To inherit bliss unending,
    Or eternity of woe. Amen.

S. MARY MAGDALENE.
(22nd July.)

200 Son of the Highest! deign to cast
  On us a pitying eye;
Thou, who repentant Magdalene
  Didst call to endless joy.

Again the royal treasury
  Receives the long lost coin;
The gem is found, and, cleans'd from mire,
  Doth all the stars outshine.

O Jesu! balm of every wound!
　The sinner's only stay!
Grant us true penitential tears
　To wash our guilt away.

Blest Saviour! hear the fervent prayer
　Which weeping we implore,
Oh! guide us through the storms of life,
　Safe to the eternal shore.

O Holy Trinity! to Thee
　Be praise and glory given,
For all the love which Thou hast shown,
　To win lost man to heaven.　Amen.

THE TRANSFIGURATION.

(6th August.)

201　How tenderly, how patiently,
　　Jesu! Thou winnest souls to Thee,
　Now for our sakes as God revealed,
　Now in deep lowliness concealed.

　By the same voice which Jesus owns,
　We too are all adopted sons;
　The glory which in Him we see,
　Is pledged to us eternally.

What hear we from the cloud above?
What on the mount doth Jesus prove?
Shadows and types were past and gone,
The truth itself remained alone.

Obedient to the Father's will,
The world's atonement to fulfil;
Once more He lays His glory by,
Returning to mortality.

O Christ! Whom now on earth we see.
Through faith's dark glass imperfectly,
Grant us, when free'd from earth's alloy,
To see Thee face to face in joy.   Amen.

---

202 O Thou, from whom all goodness flows,
    I lift my soul to Thee;
In all my sorrows, conflicts, woes,
    Good Lord, remember me.

  If on my aching burdened heart
    My sins lie heavily,
Thy pardon grant, Thy peace impart,
    Good Lord, remember me.

If trials sore obstruct my way,
   And ills I cannot flee,
Then let my strength be as my day;
   Good Lord, remember me.

If worn with pain, disease and grief,
   This feeble frame should be,
Grant patience, rest, and kind relief;
   Good Lord, remember me.

And oh, when in the hour of death
   I bow to Thy decree,
Jesu, receive my parting breath;
   Good Lord, remember me.   Amen.

THE HOLY NAME OF JESUS.

(7th August.)

[See Hymn 141.]

231

... ... unto the way
And that I am... her
Tho' let no one think to stop my day;
Good Lord remember me.

... a weary pain, disease and grief,
Thou feeble Savior should be,
... ... and find relief,
Good Lord, remember me.

And oh, when in the hour of death
I bow to Thy decree,
Jesus receive my parting breath;
Good Lord remember me.   Amen.

———

THE HOLY NAME OF JESUS.

(S. A. T.)

[See Hymn 141.]

HYMNS FOR CHILDREN.

203 We were only little babies,
　　Knowing neither good nor harm,
　When the Priest of God Most Holy
　　Took us gently in his arm.

　And he sprinkled our young faces,
　　With the water clear and bright,
　And he signed our Saviour's token
　　On our little foreheads white.

　In the Name of God the Father,
　　Of the Son and Holy Ghost,
　He baptized us then, and made us
　　Soldiers in our Master's host.

　Then we promised by our sureties,
　　Vowing for us solemnly,
　Manfully to fight His battles,
　　Gentle, kind, and good to be.

At our posts beneath His banner,
   We must watch, and strive, and pray,
By the Grace of God within us
   Growing better every day.

For the little flowers grow brightly
   In the early morning dew,
And when God's good Spirit feeds them,
   Children's hearts grow holy too.

We must keep our early promise,
   We must guard what He has given,
Till the Lord, Who loved and saved us,
   Take us to our home in Heaven.
                      Amen.

---

294   Do no sinful action,
      Speak no angry word,
   Ye belong to Jesus,
      Children of the Lord.

   Christ is kind and gentle,
      Christ is pure and true,
   And His little children
      Must be holy too.

There's a wicked spirit
    Watching round you still,
And he tries to tempt you
    To all harm and ill.

But ye must not hear him
    Though 'tis hard for you
To resist the evil,
    And the good to do.

For ye promised truly
    In your infant days,
To renounce him wholly,
    And forsake his ways.

Ye are new-born Christians,
    Ye must learn to fight
With the bad within you,
    And to do the right.

Christ is your own Master,
    He is good and true,
And His little children
    Must be holy too.   Amen.

———

We were washed in holy water,
    We were set Christ's Church within,
Gifted with His Holy Spirit,
    And forgives all our sin.

But though born again, and granted
    Grace to pray and strength to fight,
Still remains our sinful nature,
    Weakened, not extinguished quite.

Sinful thoughts of pride and passion,
    Greedy wishes, selfish cares,
In our human hearts lie hidden,
    Ready to awaken there.

Still the wrong way will seem pleasant,
    Still the right way will seem hard;
All our life we shall be tempted,
    We must ever be on guard.

We are soldiers doing battle,
    Day by day, and hour by hour,
Each one with his own temptations
    Striving in the Spirit's power.

Still that Spirit stronger groweth
    In the hearts that hold it fast;
He will help us, teach us, crown us,
    More than conquerors at the last.
                  Amen.

---

206 When we speak of the Lord Jesus,
      When His sweet Name is said,
   We will repeat it holily,
      We will bow the head.

For our Lord He is and Master,
　And He let His Father's side
He was born a little Baby,
　Here He lived and died.

'Twas for us He left His glory,
　Died the death of pain and shame;
We will try to do Him honour,
　We will love His Name.

In the holy Church we say it,
　Speaking all with one accord,
In our quiet homes we read it
　In God's Holy Word.

Jesus Christ, our Lord and Master,—
　Whensoe'er that Name is said,
We will repeat it solemnly,
　We will bow the head.

207　Once in royal David's City
　　Stood a lowly cattle shed,
　Where a mother laid her Baby,
　　In a manger for His bed.
　Mary was that mother mild,
　Jesus Christ her little child.

He came down to earth from Heaven,
  Who is God and Lord of all.
And His shelter was a stable,
  And His cradle was a stall;
With the poor, and mean, and lowly,
Lived on earth our Saviour Holy.

And through all His wondrous childhood,
  He would honour and obey,
Love and watch the lowly maiden,
  In whose gentle arms He lay.
Christian children all must be
Mild, obedient, good as He.

For He is our childhood's Pattern,
  Day by day like us He grew,
He was little, weak and helpless,
  'Tears and smiles like us He knew,
And He feeleth for our sadness,
And He shareth in our gladness.

And our eyes at last shall see Him,
  Through His Own redeeming love,
For that Child so dear and gentle
  Is our Lord in Heaven above;
And He leads His children on
To the place where He is gone.

Not in that poor lowly stable,
  With the oxen standing by,
We shall see Him; but in Heaven,
  Set at God's right Hand on high;
When like stars His children crowned,
All in white, shall wait around.   Amen.

208 There is a green hill far away,
　　Without a city wall,
Where the dear Lord was crucified
　　Who died to save us all.

We may not know, we cannot tell,
　　What pains He had to bear,
But we believe it was for us,
　　He hung and suffered there.

He died that we might be forgiven,
　　He died to make us good,
That we might go at last to Heaven,
　　Saved by His precious Blood.

There was no other good enough
　　To pay the price of sin,
He only could unlock the gate
　　Of Heaven, and let us in.

O, dearly, dearly has He loved,
　　And we must love Him too,
And trust in His redeeming blood,
　　And try His works to do.　Amen.

———

209 Little children must be quiet,
　　When to Holy Church they go,
They must sit with serious faces,
　　Must not play or whisper low.

For the Church is God's Own Temple,
  Where men go for praise and prayer,
And the Great God will not love them
  Who forget His Presence there.

They were little Jewish children,
  Who within the temple cried,
" Honour to the Son of David,"
  Standing at our Saviour's side.

How much more should Christian children,
  Know His Name and praise Him too,
Who of His Own Church are members,
  Sons of God, and born anew.

They must walk in reverent order,
  Stand for praise, and kneel for prayer,
For the Church is God's Own Temple,
  And His presence dwelleth there.

---

210 The Saints of God are holy men,
  And women good, and children dear,
All those who ever loved the Lord,
  Who live in faith and fear.

They are not all together now,
  For some are dead, and gone before,
And some are striving still on earth,
  Their trial is not o'er.

Great numbers are they of all states,
   And born in every place and land,
Who never saw each other's face,
   Nor touched each other's hand.

But they are all made one in Christ,
   They love each other tenderly,
The old and young, the rich and poor,
   Of that great company.

Christ's little children, called His Own
   And saved by His redeeming Blood,
They must be little Saints on earth,
   And all the Saints are good.

They must not fight or disobey,
   For Saints do never things like these;
They must be holy, meek, and mild,
   And try the Lord to please.

And there shall come a glorious Day,
   When all the good Saints every one,
Shall meet within their Father's home
   And stand before His Throne.
     6x.   Amen.

211 Once in baptismal waters bright
   He washed our sinful spirits white,
     Forgave us once for all.
But we have sometimes sinned since then;
Now who shall make us clean again?
     And who shall hear our call?

There is One only Who forgives,
Christ Who was born, Who died, Who lives,
     Pleading beside the Throne;
Who hath His Holy Spirit sent,
To bless that precious Sacrament
     That made us first His Own.

Who when His Holy Church within,
Confession sad of all our sin
     We make on bended knee,
Accepts the penitential prayer,
And bids His Minister declare
     Our pardon full and free.

He only hears the sinner's cry,
He only dries the mourner's eye,
     No father half so mild,
Not half so kind a mother's kiss,
When pardoning what is done amiss
     She soothes her sorrowing child.

We must take heed to cast no stain,
On souls He bought with so much pain,
     And with His Blood made pure;
And we must trust to Him alone,
Who did for all our guilt atone,
     Who made our pardon sure.

212 Do not quarrel, do not chide;
   You must love each other:
Every comrade at your side
   Is your Christian brother:
You have all been born anew,
Love and peace are fit for you.

Ye became by that new birth
   To the Lord most holy,
And His sainted ones on earth
   Peaceful are and lowly
Ye are Saints, and ye must be
Worthy of such company.

Give not back the hasty blow,
   Though 'tis given wrongly;
Let the foolish scoffer go,
   Though he tempt thee strongly;
Keep thy gentle Lord in mind,
Who was always meek and kind.

He gave back no angry word,
   When they did offend Him;
He that was the Angels' Lord,
   Called none to defend Him,
Not when hated and abused,
Scorned, and spitted on, and bruised.

But He suffered patiently
   Pain and cruel chiding;
Meek and patient you must be,
   In His Church abiding;
Pride and anger would be shame
For the Saints who bear His Name.

INDEX.

A.

	Hymn.
A Babe in Bethlehem is born	33
Abide with me, fast falls the eventide	18
Again the slowly circling year	84
A hymn for martyrs sweetly sing	38
Alike in happiness or woe	178
Alleluia, best and sweetest	45
All is o'er, the pain and sorrow	67
All people that on earth do dwell	133
All praise to Thee, my God, this night	15
All ye who seek for sure relief	145
And now the day is past and gone	192
Awake my soul and with the sun	14

B.

Before the ending of the day	125
Behold the Lamb of God	151
Be present, Holy Father	11
Be present, Holy Trinity	86

HYMN.

Bethlehem of noblest cities 47
Blest are the pure in heart 153
Blest joys for mighty wonders wrought.. 82
Blest Saviour, now thy work is done.... 79
Blessed city, heavenly Salem 113
Blessed Feasts of Blessed Martyrs 96
Brief life is here our portion 136
Brightest and best of the Sons of the Morning 40
By the Cross sad vigil keeping 66

C.

Christians awake, salute the happy morn 32
Christian soul, dost thou desire 195
Christ is gone up, yet ere he passed.... 114
Christ is made the sure foundation 113
Christ, Whose glory fills the sky 46
Come, Holy Ghost, our souls inspire ... 4
Come, Holy Ghost, with God the Son... 122
Come, Holy Ghost, our souls inspire ... 84
Come let us praise the Name of God.... 127
Come, Thou Holy Spirit, come 3
Come, Thou Redeemer of the earth 28
Conquering kings their titles take 139
Creator of the stars of night 27

D.

Daughter of Sion, cease thy bitter tears.. 49
Day of wrath, O day of mourning 23
Days and moments quickly flying 189
Disposer Supreme and Judge of the earth 93
Do no sinful action 204
Do not quarrel, do not chide 212

E.

Hymn.

Eternal Monarch, King most high...... 76

F.

Father of all, to Thee we raise......... 34
Father of Heaven, whose love profound..134
From lands that see the sun arise 34

G.

'Gainst what foemen art thou rushing...100
Glory to Thee, Who safe has kept, (Part
  iii) 14
God as on this day made the lights 129
God eternal, mighty King..............118
God moves in a mysterious way........171
God speaks the word, the floods obey...128
Great God, what do I see and hear..... 24

H.

Hail, flowerets in the martyr crown 37
Hail the day that sees him rise 78
Hail, thou once despised Jesus 198
Hark, a thrilling voice is sounding 21
Hark the glad sound, the Saviour comes. 25
Hark, the herald-angels sing 30
Heralds of Christ, through whom go
  forth 95
His trial o'er, and now beneath 63
Holy, Holy, Holy! Lord God Almighty. 89
Holiest, breathe an evening blessing....185
Holy Jesu, Saviour blessed............196

	HYMN.
Holy Spirit, Lord of Light	85
Hosanna to the living Lord	158
How sweet the name of Jesus sounds	168
How tenderly, how patiently	201

I.

If there be that skills to reckon	190
I know that my Redeemer lives	109
In stature grows the Heavenly Child	43
I worship Thee, sweet Will of God	184

J.

Jerusalem, my happy home	163
Jerusalem the Golden, (Part ii)	136
Jesus Christ is risen to day	68
Jesu, grant me this I pray	161
Jesu lives, no longer now	73
Jesu, lover of my soul	162
Jesu, meek and gentle!	142
Jesu, meek and lowly	141
Jesu, redemption all divine	77
Jesu, Refuge of the weary	193
Jesus shall reign where'er the sun	171
Jesu, the Law and Pattern whence	55
Jesu, the very thought of Thee	42
Jesu, the Virgin's Crown, do Thou	99
Jesu, the world's Redeemer, hear	98
Jesu, Who brought'st redemption nigh	75

L.

	HYMN.
Let all on earth with songs rejoice	94
Let every heart exulting beat	174
Let Saints below join Saints above	155
Light's glittering morn bedecks the sky	70
Little children must be quiet	209
Lo! from the desert homes	104
Lo! now is our accepted day	53
Lord, as to Thy dear Cross we flee	166
Lord Jesus, God and man	117
Lord of our life and God of our salvation	197
Lord, pour Thy Spirit from on high	115
Lord, when we bend before Thy Throne	58

M.

Morn of morns, and day of days	9
My God, and is Thy table spread	6
My God, how wonderful Thou art	140
My God, I love Thee, not because	182
My God, my Father, while I stray	156

N.

Nearer, my God, to Thee	177
Now that the daylight fills the sky	12

O.

O blest Creator of the light	126
O Christ, our hope, our heart's desire	81
O Christ, Who has prepared a place	80
O Father, Who didst all things make	188

	Hymn.
Oft in danger, oft in woe	160
O God of Hosts, the mighty Lord	147
O God of truth, O Lord of might	123
O God, our help in ages past	175
O God, unchangeable and true	134
O God, unseen, yet ever near	8
O Gracious hand that freely gives	180
O happy day, when first was poured	39
O help us now each hour of need	169
O Holy Lord, content to dwell	119
Oh what if we are Christ's	137
O Jesu, King most wonderful, (Part i)	i. 42
O Jesu, Thou the beauty art, (Part iii)	42
O Lord of Hosts, Whose glory fills	110
O Lord, how joyful 'tis to see	170
O Love, Who formedst me to wear	157
O Maker of the world, give ear	54
Once in baptismal waters bright	211
Once in Royal David's city	207
Once more the solemn season calls	52
On this the day that saw the earth	10
O Sion, open wide Thy gates	101
O sons redeemed this day in sin	191
O Thou from Whom all goodness flows	209
O Thou of all Thy warriors Lord	97
O Thou Who dwellest bright on high	86
O Thou Who when the world had birth	131
Our blest Redeemer, ere he breathed	135
Our limbs refreshed with slumber now	13
Our limbs with tranquil sleep refreshed	121
O what their joy and their glory must be	19
O Word of God above	111

	HYMN.
O wondrous type, O vision fair	178
O worship the King	144
O ye who followed Christ in love	54

P.

Praise my soul the King of Heaven	176
Praise the Lord, ye heavens adore him	159
Praise we the Lord this day	102

R.

Ride on, ride on in majesty	63
Rightful Prince of martyrs Thou	35
Rock of ages, cleft for me	57

S.

Saviour, when in dust to Thee	56
See from on high, arrayed in truth and grace	48
See the destined day arise	65
Sing, my tongue, the glorious battle	61
Sing we that Blest Body broken	5
Six days' labour now are past	132
Soldiers of Christ arise	164
Songs of praise the angels sang	141
Son of the Highest, deign to cast	200
Spouse of Christ, for Him contending	107
Sweet Saviour, bless us ere we go	187
Sweet the moments, rich in blessing	194
Sun of my soul, Thou Saviour dear	16

Take up thy Cross; the Saviour said ... 150
The advent of our God 20
The day is past and gone 17
The deep a twofold offering bore 13
The eternal gifts of Christ the King 9
Thee we adore, O hidden Saviour, Thee
The foe behind, the deep before 7
The life which God's Incarnate Word .. 3
The mighty hosts on high 10
There is a blessed home ....
There is a book who runs may read ....
There is a green hill far away ....
The roseate hues of early dawn 15
The Royal banners forward go 6
The Saints of God are holy men 21
The Saviour comes, no outward pomp .. 16
The strain of praise of joy and praise ... 16
The voice that breathed o'er Eden ....
The winged herald of the day ....
They come, God's messengers of love .
Thirty years among us dwelling ....
Thou Creator art possessed ....
Thou ever-blessed Trinity ....
Thrice Holy God of wondrous might ...
Through all the changing scenes of life .
Through Judah's land the Saviour walks
Till its holy hours are past ....
'Tis done, that new that heavenly birth
To Christ the Prince of Peace ....
To earth descending, word sublime..... 2
To thee, O dear, dear country, (Part ii) 13

	Hymn.
To the name of our Salvation	154
To the Paschal Victim	72

V.

Virgin born, we bow before Thee	103

W.

Wake and lift up thyself my heart	14
We love the place, O God	149
We were only little babies	203
We were washed in holy water	205
What star is this with beams so bright	41
When Christ the Lord would come on earth	26
When I survey the wondrous Cross	59
When our tongues are bowed with woe	148
When we speak of the Lord Jesus	206
While shepherds watched their flocks by night	29
Who are these, like stars appearing	108
With Christ we share a mystic grave	1
With gentle voice the angels gave	71
Wouldst thou enjoy the eternal years	186

Y.

Ye boundless realms of Joy	183
Ye choirs of New Jerusalem	69
Ye servants of the Lord	167

www.ingramcontent.com/pod-product-compliance
Lightning Source LLC
Chambersburg PA
CBHW032137230426
43672CB00011B/2367